Table of Contents

Introduction

Thank you for investing in this book.

If you apply what you will learn in this book, then you will get clients and get paid.

A word of warning:

Freelancing is not as easy as having a job. I'm not saying that your job right now is easy, but freelancing takes a different level of commitment.

Unlike having a traditional job, with freelancing you don't have any guarantee that the money will come every 2 weeks. In freelancing, you get work or you don't get paid. Your income per month is tied by the value you are providing to your customers.

If you are ready to embark a challenging but rewarding journey then freelancing is for you.

The Truth About Freelancing

Before I tell you the way to make money as a freelancer, I want to tell you the truth behind freelancing. I don't want you to get the misconception that freelancing is easy or freelancing is super hard. It really depends on you and your work ethic.

I'm not trying to scare or anything but I just want you to be prepare because the journey will be a journey with up and downs.

The good news is if you persevere and work hard, the rewards will outweigh any cons on freelancing.

The way I recommend that you get started is to choose one of the ways to make money as a free lancer and get good at it. After making a bit of money in that skill set, you can now expand and learn other skills. Don't go jump from opportunity to opportunity. If you're really strap for cash, that the only reason I would advice you to take any job that you can get.

In the first half of this book, you will learn my top 10 ways of making money as a freelancer. On the second half of this book, I'm going to show you the best ways to find long term clients who will pay you over and over again. In addition, you will learn the closely guarded secrets of the top freelancers in the world.

I'm very excited for you so let's go straight to the first part of this book.

10 Ways To Make Money As A Freelancer

1. Fiverr

Fiverr is like the Walmart of skills and talents. If you are just starting out then fiverr is perfect for you.

You can sell almost anything here.

Can you draw? Sell it. Can you sing? Sell it. Can you video yourself and make a testimonial? Sell it.

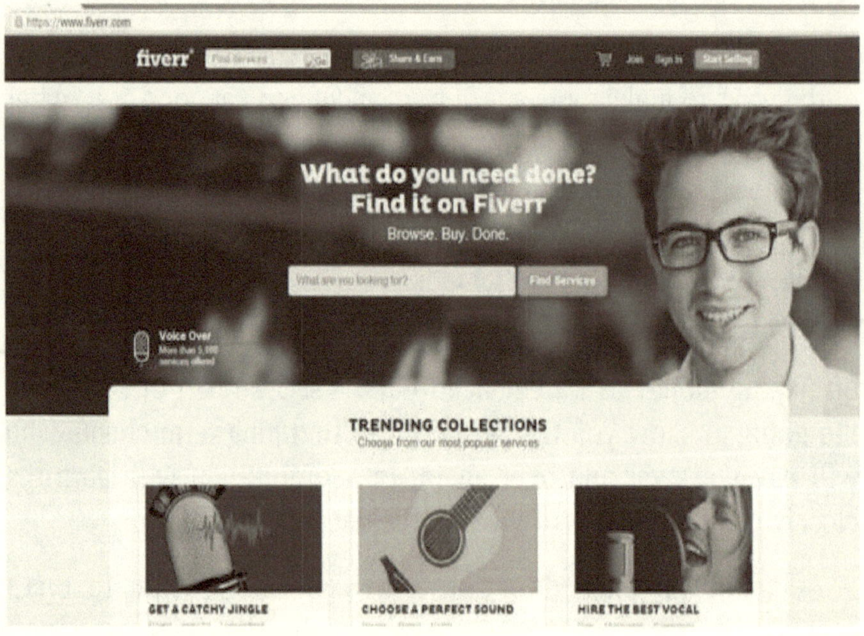

You can go to fiverr right now and literally make money an hour later.

Search for any skills you have or any skill/product you are interested in and see if there are people selling the same thing. If there are lots of people selling that skill/product then you can certainly make money selling it!

I can go to fiverr right now, type “seo article” and there are hundreds of people selling their seo writing services.

Sell what you know and you'll make money here.

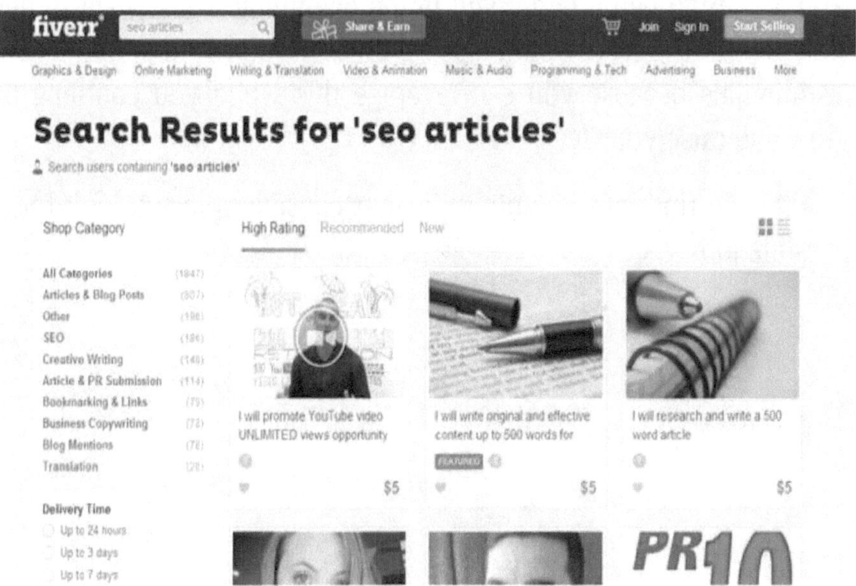

Create a free account at http://fiverr.com to get started.

2. Writing articles

Article writing is one of the oldest ways to make money as a freelancer. And it still works today! There is still a huge demand for people who can write quality content.

If you have any talent or interest in writing articles then article writing could be perfect for you. You can choose from different topics like Business, marketing, seo, consulting, social media, relationship, medicine and many more. The topics are endless!

If I'm just getting started then I would register at elance.com first and find my first few clients there. I really wouldn't mind being underpaid in the beginning. I just want to get experience at first. It would also be great if you could gather a few testimonials because you can leverage this while you continue to grow and raise your fees.

To find jobs, simply type your chosen topic and look for a possible job.

real estate writer

Freelancers | Portfolio Samples | **Jobs**

Post Your Job

All Jobs / real estate writer (69 results) 

Sort by: Posted Date ▾

Results for 'real estate writer'

Re-write article for Real Estate Photography blog

Fixed Price: Less than $500 | Posted: 32 minutes ago | Ends: 14d, 23h | **0** Proposals

I need professional writer to re-write articles related to Real Estate Photo/Video services. I will provide you links to various articles to rework. Articles must be - 700 to 1000 words in length - writte... ▾

Category: Article Writing   Skills: Blog Writing, Article Rewriting

| b****man | Canada

Local Contributor for NJ Real Estate Blog

Fixed Price: Less than $500 | Posted: 9h, 35m ago | Ends: 14d, 14h | **1** Proposal

Writing and grammar, knowledge of real estate, Jersey City and surrounding area Job Description: We are a Jersey City real estate blog looking for local writers to contribute to our site. We focus on sales... ▾

Category: Web Content   Skills: Blogs, Writing   Preferred Location: United States

| h****208 | United States

writer needed to rewrite content for real estate website network

Fixed Price: Less than $500 | Posted: 11h, 44m ago | Ends: 12h, 15m | 23 Proposals

Get any job you can get for now then expand once you got those few dollars and testimonials. Those testimonials are a big consideration for business owners who want to hire a freelancer. Also, always try to get a higher rating and good feedback from your customers. Take care of them and they will take care of you.

3. Web Design

If you know how to code or love designing websites then this is for you. This job pays a much higher rate compared to article writing and selling on fiverr.

Depending on your skill level and the job requirement, a job may take from an hour to more than 5 hours. Web designers can also leverage their work by putting their name and website link in the footer of the client's site. Make sure that you tell the owner of the site before doing any of that. If he agrees then put, if not then just don't do it.

You can sign up in upwork (former odesk.com) and get sarted fairly quickly.

If you want to be a web designer but still have no skills yet then I recommend that you sign up with some courses on udemy.com. Some are free and some are paid.

Go to – http://upwork.com

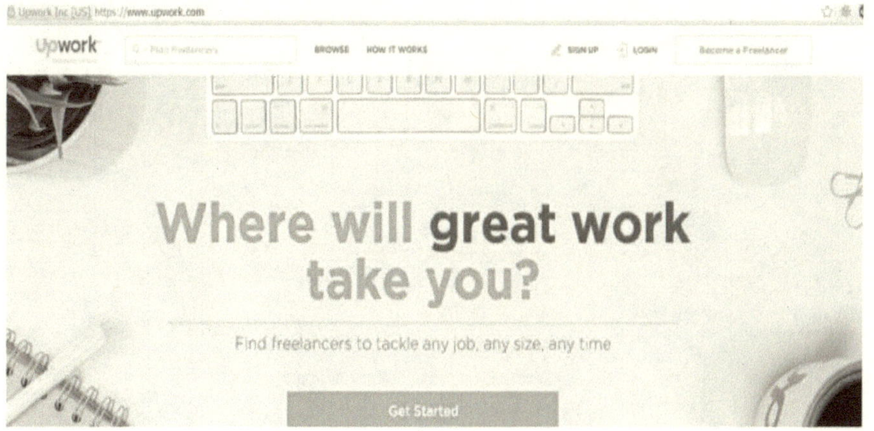

Take courses at http://udemy.com

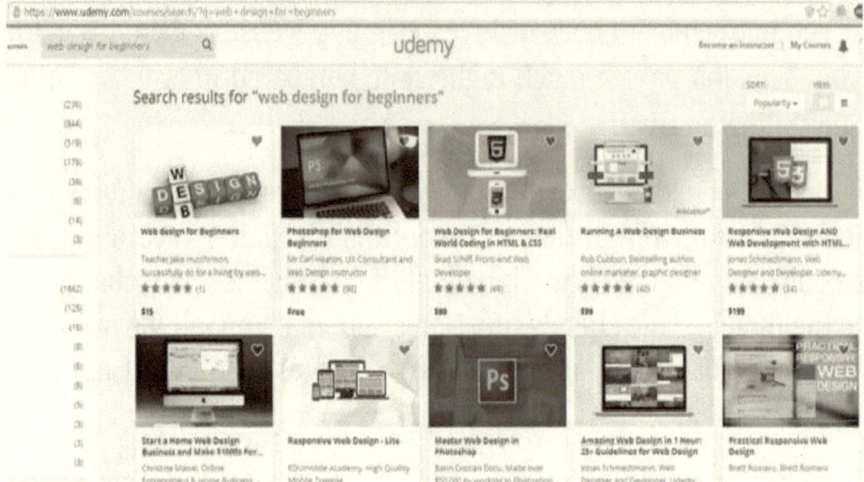

4. Search Engine Optimization

In SEO, you can either be an seo article writer or a link builder.

Both pays really well especially if you can follow your clients instructions on what they want with an article or with link building.

Also, if you have been doing a great job for a client then there is a possibility that you are the one who's going to get the first call every time he needs an article. I recommend that you take your first job seriously and provide the best quality that you can provide.

Remember that the best way to get new clients is to take care of of current clients.

You can also use elance.com, fiverr.com and upwork.com to find jobs about SEO.

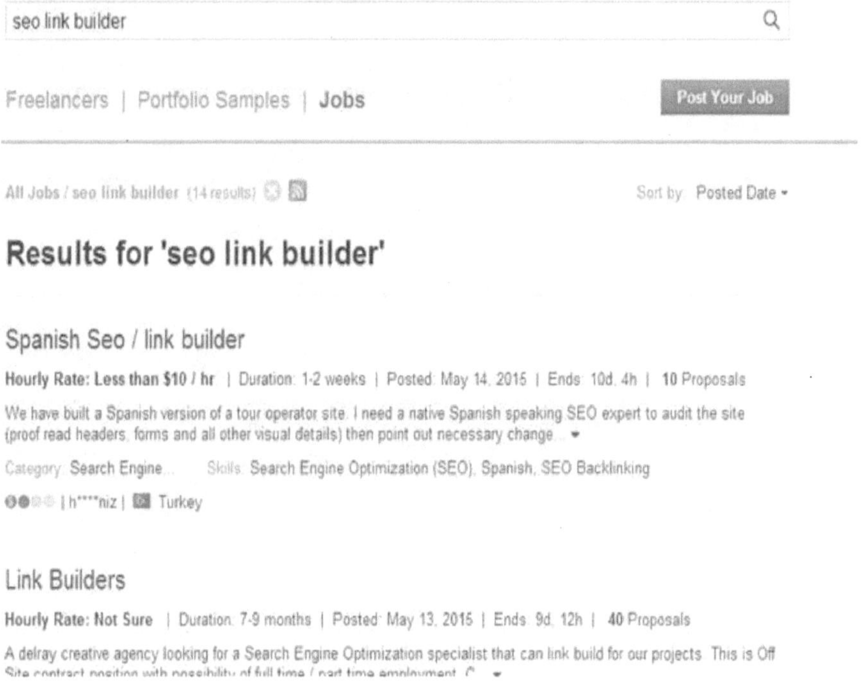

seo link builder

Freelancers | Portfolio Samples | **Jobs**

Post Your Job

All Jobs / seo link builder (14 results)

Sort by Posted Date

Results for 'seo link builder'

Spanish Seo / link builder

Hourly Rate: Less than $10 / hr | Duration: 1-2 weeks | Posted: May 14, 2015 | Ends: 10d, 4h | **10** Proposals

We have built a Spanish version of a tour operator site. I need a native Spanish speaking SEO expert to audit the site (proof read headers, forms and all other visual details) then point out necessary change...

Category: Search Engine... Skills: Search Engine Optimization (SEO), Spanish, SEO Backlinking

| h****niz | Turkey

Link Builders

Hourly Rate: Not Sure | Duration: 7-9 months | Posted: May 13, 2015 | Ends: 9d, 12h | **40** Proposals

A delray creative agency looking for a Search Engine Optimization specialist that can link build for our projects. This is Off Site contract position with possibility of full time / part time employment. C...

5. Writing non fiction books

This job requires a bit more work on the research part because a book is much much longer than an article. Also, the grammar errors (or the lack of it) of your book would be a huge selling point of your skills.

If you are good at research and can structure a whole idea and break it down into pieces then writing non-fiction ebooks is for you.

Also, I recommend that you stick to a topic that you already have background about. If you worked as a Financial Planner in the past then you could write something about saving and investing money. I usually stick with the topics that I have some interest with because I have a hard time writing something that I don't fully understand.

If you're good at research then there wouldn't be any problems for you.

non fiction ebook

Freelancers | Portfolio Samples | **Jobs** Post Your Job

All Jobs / non fiction ebook (79 results) Sort by: Posted Date

Results for 'non fiction ebook'

Long Term Working Relationship (eBook Writer Needed)

Fixed Price: $100 - $110 | Posted: 8h, 33m ago | Ends: 14d, 15h | **11** Proposals

I am looking to create a series of books within the occult niche. This includes Witchcraft, Wicca, Magick, Paganism and so on. The books will be 8'000 - 10,000 words long with the first one being 10,000 wo...

Category: E-books and Blogs Skills: Ghostwriting, Non-Fiction Writing, Content Writing

| u****s96 | United Kingdom

Experienced writer required for Fitness related ebooks

Fixed Price: About $50 | Posted: 13h, 34m ago | Ends: 14d, 10h | **6** Proposals

European publishing company is aiming to establish lasting relationships with professional ghostwriters. Details: -Non Fiction writers required to work on assignments covering an array of topics in the heal...

Category: E-books and Blogs Skills: Non-Fiction Writing, WordPerfect, Academic Writing

| F****ing | Ireland

Write HOW TO and STEP BY STEP e-books in NON-FICTION from a Woman'

6. Writing non fiction books

If you are a creative one and you enjoy writing stories then this is perfect for you. There are tons of book right now being self-published by virtually unknown authors.

Two of the most famous genres today are ROMANCE and EROTICA.

With the rise of “50 Shades Of Grey”. A lot of writers/publishers are taking
advantage of this trend and are writing and/or outsourcing their books to freelancers.

This is a golden opportunity for you because the demand right now is so high, readers especially teens just can't get enough of these books.

Just take a look at amazon.com and see how famous these books are, there are hundreds of new titles every day and the market is still not saturated.

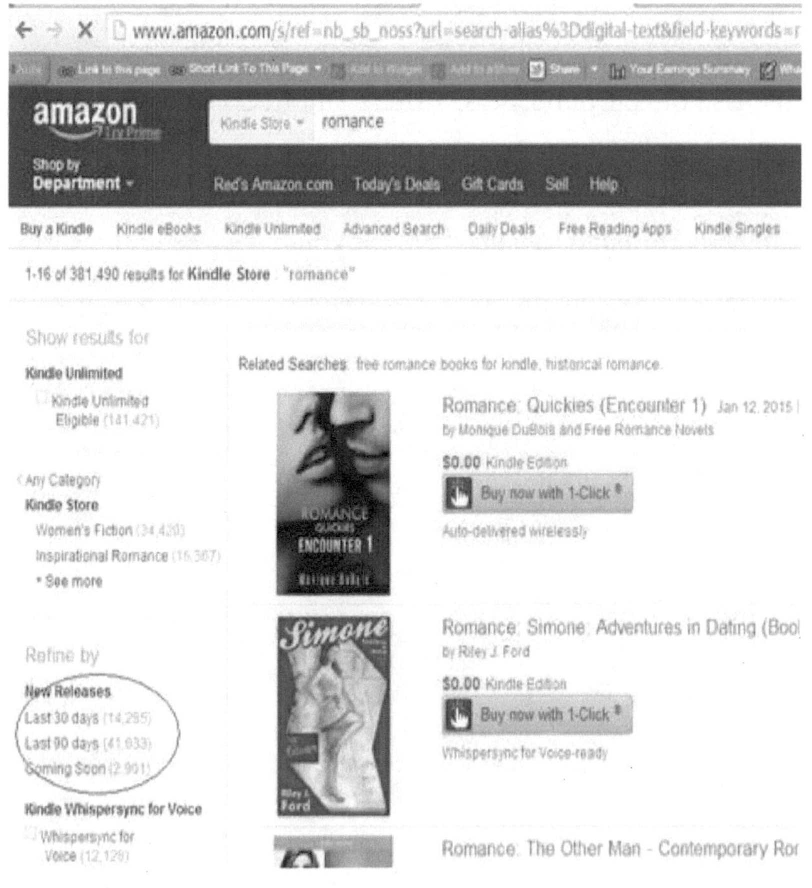

You can still participate in this gold rush, it's not yet over and I believe it will still last a good 3-4 years. Go get your share of that gold and start writing.

7. Logo and ebook cover designer

With the rise of self publishers, writers and freelancers in general, the ebook cover and logo design continues to benefit. If you know how to edit book covers and create logos then this can be a very lucrative and profitable freelance job for you.

You can go to websites like 99designs and fiverr.com to sell your book covers.

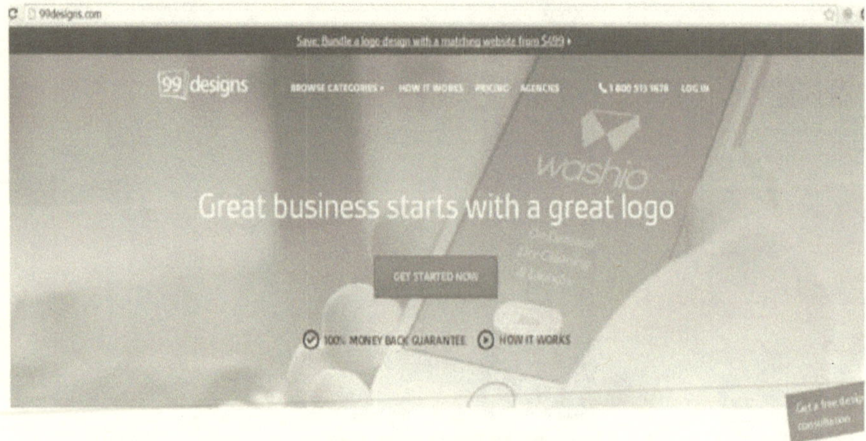

If you want to make more money then I suggest you create your own website selling book cover design.

Here are some of my favorite book covers to get inspiration from:

TOMORROW
McENROE
LOSE WEIGHT THROUGH GREAT SEX WITH CELEBRITIES
(the Elvis way)
JOHN UPDIKE
NEW
NEW
MICHAEL LEWIS

ROBERT
HUGHES
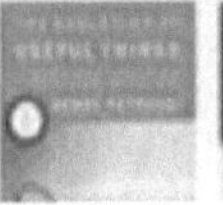

8. Resume Writer

This is one of the best ways to get started because you can easily research what makes a great resume and apply it. You can literally learn how to do this in less than an hour and make money the next day. You just have to be willing to do the work and ask for work!

People are still paying for this even though it seems easy to do. Also, a resume is an important document that's why charging a good amount of money for it is a no brainer.

If you want to write an awesome resume then I recommend that you read my short book about it. It's called "The Perfect Resume", you can easily found it on amazon.com or on kindle.

Resumes have already change and plain, ugly looking resumes don't work anymore. There's a new kind of resume and I reveal that inside my book.

Anyway, if the client is asking for a "normal" resume then go write your normal looking resume. But it can never hurt to suggest writing the new way.

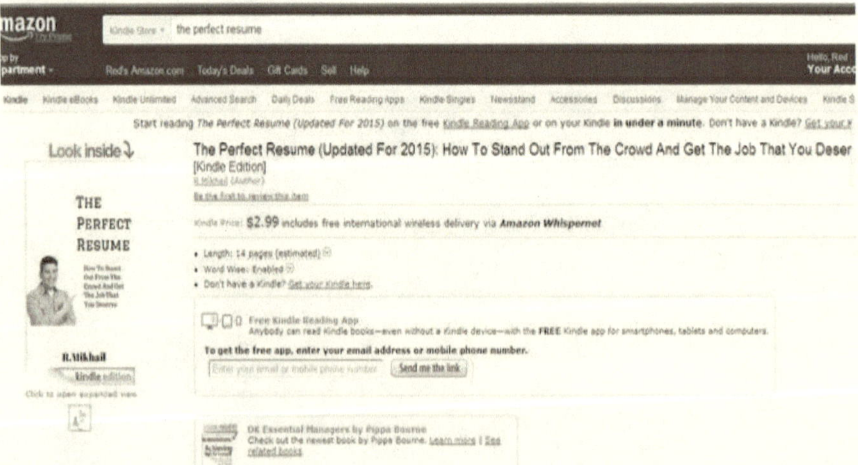

9. Freelance/Blogger Combo

As a freelance and a blogger, you can write about your passion, hobbies and interest. Overtime, if you provide amazing and non-boring content, you will grow your following. You can sell to these people and make a decent amount of money.

One example of this is Fran Kerr of http://highonclearskin.com

She suffers from pimples and acne in the past and decided to find a solution for it. She then shares these solutions on her blog and slowly build followers and readers. Her readers started asking a lot of question and she figured that she can't answer them all but if she write a book about it then she can help a lot of people.

If you have any passion, interest or hobbies that you would like to share then this opportunity might suit you.

To get started, you can register a domain name at Godaddy.com and a hosting in hostgator.com

10. Copywriting

If you're a beginner and need the money this week. Then don't choose this one.

Copywriting can be very lucrative and very profitable but it does take more work and studies to master. In fact, you can't even master it, you can only hope to try.

If you have no idea what copywriting is, it means writing advertisement for products.

Here are some example of great copies that sold millions of dollars of products worth.

The first example below sells a dvd course about golf.

You can find the whole ad here:

http://swiped.co/file/55-year-old-golfer-ad-by-john-carlton/

If petite women and 12-year-old kids are using this secret to hit perfect drives over 250 yards... imagine what it can do for YOU!

How Does An Out-Of-Shape 55 Year-Old Golfer, Crippled By Arthritis & 71 Lbs. Overweight, Still Consistently Humiliate PGA Pros In Head-To-Head Matches By Hitting Every Tee Shot Further And Straighter Down The Fairway?

The answer will shock and delight you! It's an amazingly simple

If you want to learn more about copywriting, I highly recommend these books and blogs:

http://www.john-carlton.com/
http://www.thegaryhalbertletter.com/
http://www.copyblogger.com/

The Ultimate Sales Letter: Attract New Customers. Boost your Sales by Dan Kennedy

Scientific Advertising by Claude Hopkins

Ogilvy On Advertising by David Ogilvy

How to Find Long Term Clients via LinkedIn

This training for LinkedIn works whether you're a freelancer or consultant.

Apply what you'll learn and I believe that you will make money freelancing, keep clients and make more money on the long term.

Profile Creation - The Right Way

Your profile can make or break your business.

It is the first thing people see when they click on your name.

To be honest with you, I don't even try to stand out. I just make my profile as simple and clean looking as possible.

The Basics

Note: If you already have an account and you feel like you don't need to read this part then you can skip this part and go to the next chapter "Adding Connections".

If you don't have an account yet, then go to http://LinkedIn.com and register for a free account.

Step 1 - Your Photo

Make your photo as professional as possible. A white or blue background will do.

Here are some great pictures to model from.

Step 2 - Headline

Your headline should define your business or whatever it is you are trying to sell.

Examples:

- Selling his consulting practice

Jack Welch

Executive Chairman, The Jack Welch Management Institute

- selling his seo services

Kotton Grammer

Nationally Recognized Search Engine Optimization Expert

Step 3 - Education and Experience

I only have one rule when it comes to putting education and experience in my Linkedin. It has to be connected to whatever your practice is today. SO if you are selling marketing consultancy then put your experience related to your business today. If it's not related, then don't bother putting it on Linkedin.

In the experience part, write exactly what you did in your past jobs or business ventures.

Here's a pretty good example.

Assistant Project Manager

Cobalt Construction LLC

July 2009 – August 2009 (2 months)

Seem mostly that I got cussed at a lot while developing construction bids for mid scale commercial construction projects and doing plan take offs. Researched engineering solutions and subcontractors for specialized construction projects throughout the southwest United States.

Insurance Adjuster

Wardlaw Claims

August 2008 – October 2008 (3 months)

Insurance Adjuster for National Disaster Area created by Hurricane Ike

Owner- Consulatant

Geoscape GIS

March 2006 – June 2008 (2 years 4 months) | Huntington Beach, CA

Utility Scale Renewable energy development. Siting and feasibility for wind and solar installations. Project management and planning of energy transmission projects including $1.5B Sunrise Powerlink in southern California. Software development of ROW real estate database software to manage and value engineer ROW projects; the first of it's kind in the industry.

Contractor

Self Employed

March 2007 – December 2007 (10 months)

Home Improvement Contractor in Dallas, TX

Here's another one.

Adviser and Shareholder

Sons & Co.

April 2014 – Present (1 year 3 months)

With 125 years of collective experience, Sons & Co. have an exemplary track-record and continue to exceed client's expectations by producing the world's most luxurious and dignified homes in London's most exclusive addresses.

With commercial awareness, distinguished development experience and an institutional approach- the management team expertly guide projects through each phase of acquisition, development and design on behalf of discerning clients and investors

Partner

eMoov.co.uk

December 2013 – Present (1 year 7 months)

eMoov are the UK's largest low cost, fixed fee online estate agent. Since formation in 2010 they have sold over £250 million worth of property and saved property sellers over £6m in fees.

Estate agency has long awaited disruption to the mystique of finding buyers and guiding people through the home moving process. eMoov.co.uk are innovating the property industry by providing a low cost solution to selling across England, Scotland and Wales. .

Partner

Leadership and Management Ltd.

July 2013 – Present (2 years)

Leadership and management (L+M) are an innovative and entrepreneurial project and construction consultancy that brings inspirational leadership and management to a wide range of capital investment and asset management projects. Great believers in driving value, as well as cost, L+M deploy the right resources and apply the very best technical expertise to their clients' projects from day one.

Step 4 - Summary

This is different from experience and education.

It's basically an elevator speech on what your business is all about.

I try to make it as simple and straight to the point.

Here's my very own summary for my profile.

Summary

Helping Businesses And Professionals 10X Their Profits.

If Your Looking For Quality SEO or Quality Social Media Management, You've Come To The Right Place.

Step 5 - Add Your Skills

Make sure that you'll add your skills in your profile.

Step 6 - Recommendations

Later I'm going to show you how you can get recommendations. For now, just know that this is one of the most important part of your profile.

▾ 2 recommendations

Zach Punnett
President at Punnett Construction

Joshua is a dedicated business professional that uses his extreme intellectual capabilities not only to further himself but... View↓

Paul Ikin
Relationship Executive - helping organi...

Joshua is a true professional and one of the best GIS experts I have had the pleasure of working with. I would not hesitate... View↓

Adding Connections

In the past, I always suggest that people add as many connections as possible. Today, I'm a bit more choosy about it. I make sure that everyone whom I will connect to is a potential client. It means that whoever he is, his profile should be related to whoever my target market is.

Let's say you're a marketing consultant for Ophthalmologist. Then obviously, I should only add doctors or ophthalmologist as connection.

Where To Find Connections

Step 1 - Think about your target market

Ask yourself this question.

Who is my target market and where can I possibly
find them?

For me personally, my target people are plastic surgeons and ophthalmologists.

So how do you do it?

SIMPLE.

Just search for job/person titles with your keyword on it.

In my case I'm looking for plastic surgeons.

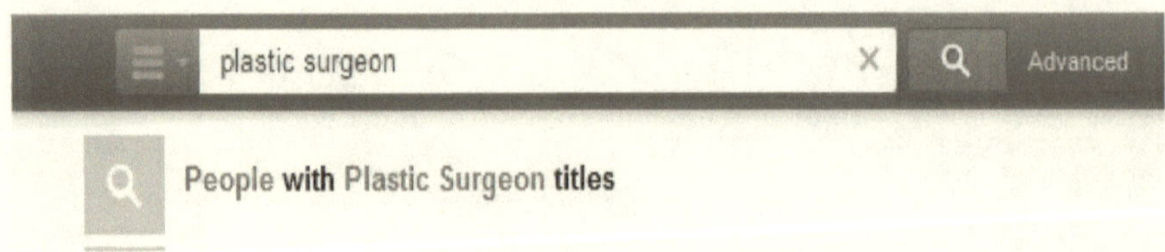

Click it and you'll see plastic surgeons.

Add them as connections.

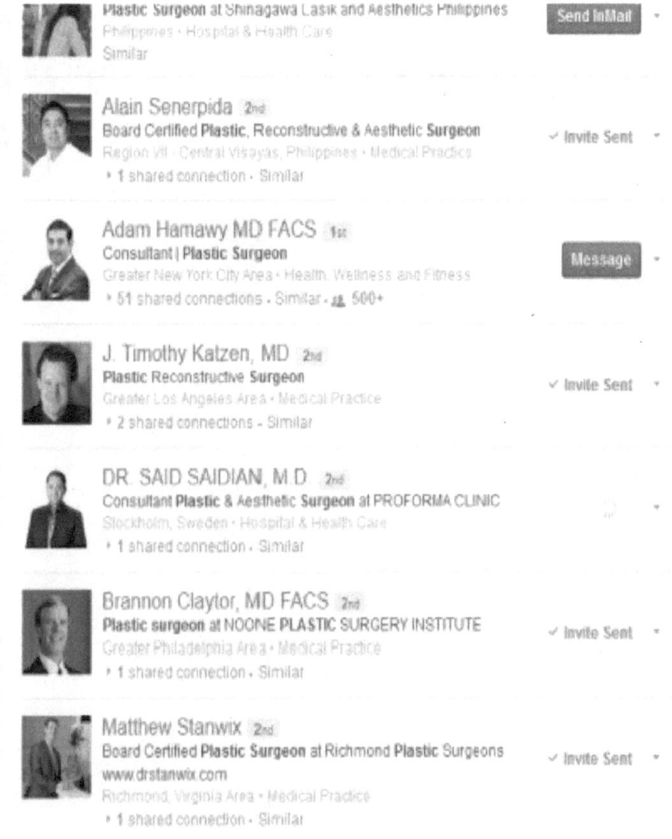

Some people are not allowed to be added directly. You can message them and ask any question about their type of surgery and ask to connect.

Add as many connections as possible. (connections that are related to your business)

NEVER EVER SELL ANYTHING WHEN YOU'RE JUST ON THE BEGINNING STAGE OF YOUR RELATIONSHIP.

Hot Tip: If you're clients are all over the place, like if it doesn't matter if they are doctors, dentist, plumbers etc. An amazing thing to do is to get their own services. Hire them as your plumber, as your personal doctor etc. Once you are already their client,it'll be much easier to sell to them and pitch your service.

Join Groups/Businesses

One of the most effective ways to find clients through Linkedin is by joining groups or business establishments.

To search for groups, just type on the search box whatever it is you're trying to find.

Do not hit enter immediately, a drop down will appear instead.

Join or Follow the group and look at its members.

Then add them as connection.

16 results

Current Company: Richmond Plastic Surgeons × 

Matthew Stanwix 2nd

Board Certified **Plastic** Surgeon at **Richmond Plastic Surgeons**

www.drstanwix.com

Richmond, Virginia Area • Medical Practice

▸ **1** shared connection • Similar

Connect

LinkedIn Member

RN at **Richmond Plastic Surgeons**,Inc

United States • Cosmetics

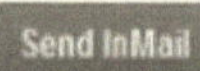

Kit Young in

Administrator and Director of Information Systems at **Richmond Plastic Surgeons**

Richmond, Virginia Area • Hospital & Health Care

Similar

Connect

Current: Administrator and Director of Information Systems at **Richmond P**...

Past: Director of IT and clinical outcomes at **Richmond** Gastroenterolo...

EMR Deployment Analyst for Independent Physicians Program at ...

EHR Project Management at Virginia Diabetes and Endocrinology

Isaac Wornom 3rd

Plastic Surgeon and partner at **Richmond Plastic Surgeons**

Richmond, Virginia Area • Medical Practice

Similar

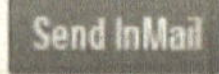

LinkedIn Member

office manager at **Richmond Plastic Surgeons**

Richmond, Virginia Area • Plastics

Send InMail

Lewis Ladocsi 3rd

plastic surgeons | Advanced

plastic surgeons

American Society of Plastic Surgeons
Nonprofit Organization Management; 51-200 employees

Australian Society of Plastic Surgeons
Nonprofit Organization Management; 1-10 employees

Plastic Surgeons **of Istanbul**
Health, Wellness and Fitness; 1-10 employees

Lexington Plastic Surgeons**/Dr. Michael E. Jones**
Medical Practice

Richmond Plastic Surgeons
Health, Wellness and Fitness; 51-200 employees

Marketing for Plastic Surgeons

Facial Plastic **& Reconstructive** surgeons **(FPRS)**

Lexington Plastic Surgeons
Cosmetic Surgical & Non-Invasive Treatments

Certified Plastic Surgeons
Lead Generator at Certified Plastic Surgeons

Plastic Surgeons
Owner, New Zealand Institute of Plastic and Cosmetic Surgery

BAPRAS Association of Plastic Surgeons
Association of Plastic Reconstructive & Aesthetic Surgeons in the Balkan Region

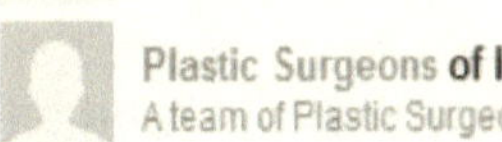

Plastic Surgeons **of Istanbul**
A team of Plastic Surgeons

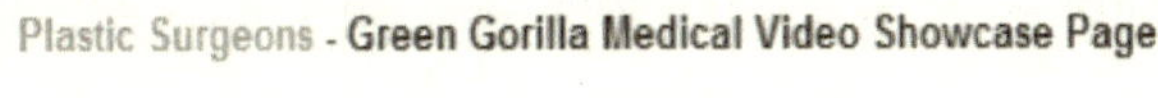

Plastic Surgeons - **Green Gorilla Medical Video Showcase Page**

Profile Trust Building

It's going to be all about building trust through your profile.

The best trust builder that you need are

PLUS ON SKILLS/ENDORSEMENTS and RECOMMENDATIONS…

A. SKILLS/ENDORSEMENTS

This is not as important as the recommendations but still it is nice to get a few plus on your skills. What I would do is I'll spend a good 30 minutes just endorsing other people. I usually get a pretty good amount of counter-endorsements just by doing this.

To endorse a person, simple click their skills and it'll automatically add to their number of skills/endorsements.

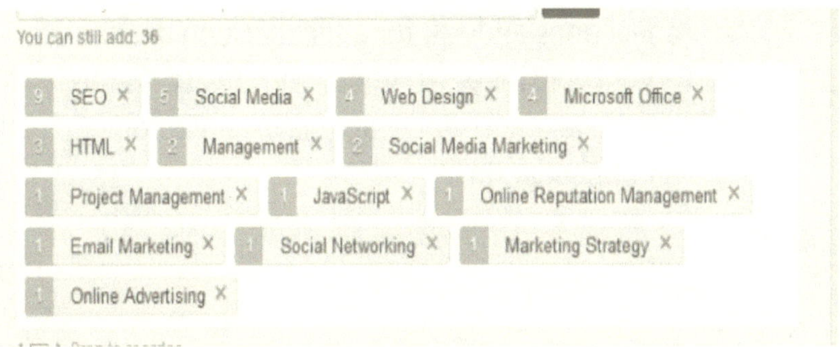

B. Recommendations

▾ 5 recommendations, including:

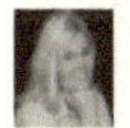

Kara Steck
--Search Engine Optimization Expert

I have a friend who happens to be an Optical surgeon and I decided to refer him to Red since I know that one of his... View↓

Deon Bryan
Reputation SEO Consultant For Business Owners. Is It True What's Being Said About You Online? Find Out With Free Report.

Working with Red has got to be the best decision I have ever made. His work ethic is second to none. Just a genuinely good... View↓

3 more recommendations↓

This is the holy grail of profile trust building.

A lot of clients are always asking for recommendations. If you have tons of recommendations then you'll be able to counter their objections and get them as your clients.

Also, if a lot of your clients are saying that "you are the best", "you do quality work" then you'll be able to build more trust for your consulting business.

So how do you get recommendations?

A. Add past and present clients as connections

The very first thing I do is add past and present clients as

connections and ask for a feedback on my service.
If your business is good and really helped a lot of customers then you want have any problem getting a recommendation.

Experience

Partner
Abacus Group
October 2000 – Present (14 years 9 months) | New York, NY

Prior to my career in Executive Search, I was a Financial Officer / Controller @ MetLife, joining them after spending 5 years with Merrill Lynch and nearly 3 years as an Auditor with Pricewaterhouse.

▾ 8 recommendations, including:

Manuel C.
SEC Reporting at Voya Financial™

Laurie was instrumental in assisting me in my career search. As a fellow CPA, she understands the industry and the... View↓

Tatyana Hixon CPA
Tsquare Consulting Inc. Co-founder

Laurie was straight and to the point and showed knowledge and understanding of the industry and as well as my situation... View↓

6 more recommendations↓

In addition, make sure that they'll add your their recommendation on the correct job or your current business.

B. Request for One

Once you start doing what I will teach you in the next chapter, you'll be able to confidently request a recommendation

(since you will genuine help them in whatever it is their trying to achieve, more on this later)

C. Blackhat

Another way to do this is by trading recommendations. Now, I'm not sure if this is legal on Linkedin's terms or not. If you're going to trade recommendations, make sure that what you will write is TRUE.

Chapter 4 - How To Get Customers... The Non Salesy, Non Pressured Way.

So we created our profile,add connections, got our skills endorsed and we got our recommendations set up.

It's time to sell our services WITHOUT actually selling it.

Here's the exact step by step process on how to do this.

Step 1 - Choose my potential clients

Firstly, I would choose my potential clients and write their names on a piece of paper.

Step 2 - Know what they want and provide it

Secondly, I will think about the best way to help them solve their problems and help them get their wants and their needs.

Example:

Let's say you are targeting plumbers who may want to get more clients. (assuming you are a marketing consultant)
What I would do is I will create a pdf report about "How to get more clients for your plumbing business, spend less time on it and make more money!"

It can be as short as a 10 page report with good information about client getting for Plumbers.

In the end of the report, I will input something like this.

If this report helped you in some way or another, you

can schedule a free 30 minute 1 on 1 consulting with me! Don't worry cause I ain't gonna pitch you my services. I'll just help you with your business, create a plan of attack and if you want me to help you implement it then we'll do work together. If you're not a perfect fit or you want to implement the plan yourself, then no hurt feelings, we'll move on and I wish you all the best for your business.

I only accept 1 client per month so if you're up for the free consultation, then simply go to this link (http://yourwebsite.com) and schedule a consultation date.

Sign up while there are still spots left.
Click this link: http://youwebsite.com

Step 3 - Message Them

Message them and tell them that you have a free report you are giving away especially for plumbers (if your clients are plumbers)

Here's an example of a sample message that I would send.

Hey Mike,

Subject line: *Nothing for Sale*

Message Body:

Hi Mike,

First of all there's nothing for sale in this message. I'm a marketing consultant and I thought that the best way to get clients is to genuinely help them in their business. So that's what I'm trying to do.

I wrote a free 15 report about

"How to get more clients for your plumbing business, spend less time on it and make more money!"

Here's what you'll learn in this report.

- *benefit 1*
- *benefit 2*
- *benefit 3*
- *benefit 4*

If you want to get this report, you can download it here

(give link to the download page)

Thanks Mike!

Step 4 - Follow Up

If they did not respond after 4-5 days, then follow up and tell them about the report again.

If they did not respond again, wait for 2 weeks and message them again. If there's still not respond, then it's time to abandon ship and move on.

21 Other Ways To Find Clients

This is the ultimate resource list for beginners. It's almost impossible not to find a client if you persevere and take action.

Sign up for a free account and start building your profile. Make it as professional and as complete as possible. In addition, put as much experience as you have in your profile.

The Ultimate Resource:

1.Upwork.com

2. Elance.com

3. Fiverr.com

4. Referral from family and friends

5. Ask your office mates for possible work (if you have one)

6. Ask referral from current clients

7. 99designs.com – for logo designers

8. Flexjobs

9. Freelancer.com

10. guru.com/d/jobs/

11. krop.com – creating professional websites

12. Craigslist.com

13. getacoder.com/

14. jobs.smashingmagazine.com/

15. www.ifreelance.com/

16. peopleperhour.com/

17. workhoppers.com/en/

18. journalismjobs.com/job-listings

19. freelancewritinggigs.com/

20. jobs.problogger.net/ - for internet marketers

21. Find a BIG TIME writer and work under him, they could be the mentor that can help you achieve your freelancing goals.

6 Secrets of Successful Freelancing

1. Never ever miss a deadline

If there is only one secret to successful freelancing then this must be it. Do not accept a job if you know you can't finish it on time. You might get the first paycheck but your reputation will suffer thus dragging your freelance dreams down the drain.

Always estimate how long it will take you to finish a job and see if you can finish it on time.

Another rule of thumb is always thinking that "your reputation is better than a paycheck". If you ever have to choose from one, choose your reputation.

2. Do not over commit

This one is connected to the first secret. If you know that you can't finish a job then don't accept it. When it comes to your "to do list", do not put too much stuff into it. I usually write just 3-6 items on my to do list every day. Don't make the mistake of feeling that you have to finish 10-20 task every day to feel productive.

I would rather do 3 items that I did with quality than 10 items without much quality put into it.

3. Keep Your Sanity

As a freelancer, you are most likely to feel burnout with all the work and the stress it may bring. Remember to always schedule a break time where you will do something completely unrelated to your job.

Here are my suggestions:

A. Exercise for 30 minutes a day
B. Have a massage once or twice a week
C. use the 60-15-60 rule
 - Work for 60 minutes, then go rest for 15 minutes – go out of your house and breathe some fresh air, then go back to work again for 60 minutes.

4. Horde some money

Save 6-12 months worth of money that can avail you to not work for that span. No, I will not suggest that you stop working. You will not use this money for anything, what this will do is to put you in the position of power. Because you know you have this money on the side, you will never be afraid to walk away from a job. You never have to beg for that 1 job because you know it will not break or make you.

By doing this, you'll be able to make make smart decisions that may affect your career in the long term.

You will never be in a desperate vibe, clients smell this desperation from a mile and they will take advantage of it. If you save some money then you are already 10 steps ahead of them.

5. Follow the "No Job Is Easy" Principle

Never ever tell the client that you can finish the job in a snap! Even if you can!

If the client is expecting it in 3 days then submit it on day 3 or day 2, if you finish it 2 hours after you got hired and submit it to him,

then he will not value your work.
He will think that your work must not have quality since you finished it so fast.

Always make it appear that you slaved over your work. Your client will value it more knowing that you sweat blood and tears over their project.

6. Find a Mentor

If you can find someone who is in the position you want to be in the future, do everything you can to be mentored by him/her.

A good mentor will cut your learning curve in half and will always guide you along the way. You can also avoid "million dollar" mistakes by learning from his "million dollar failures".

Go get that mentor!

Conclusion

Thank you for reading this book and I wish that you'll have an amazing freelance career. Remember to persevere and sooner or later, you will get the results that you are looking for. Always provide value to clients and do what you are asked for. Make your clients happy and you will never be jobless again.

To your success,

AMAZON PUBLISHING BLUEPRINT

(Updated With New Marketing Module)

How to Publish Books and Make $1,000 Per Month on Amazon
Even If You Are Not a Writer

Jacob Arroyo

Table of Contents

Introduction

If you want to make extra money from home, then this book is for you.

Maybe you want to quit your job and start an online business.
Heck, you probably even tried a million "home based" business ideas, but it never worked.

If you are in any of those positions, then this book will be a life saver for you.

I remember the feeling of proving to myself that it is possible to really make money online – it was one of the best feelings in the world!

I didn't make my first $1,000 online via Kindle Publishing and it took me 3 years to do it! Insane! I'm writing this book because I believe that Kindle publishing is one of the easiest ways to make your first $1,000 online. In fact, it took me only 60 days to get to that level.

On the next page, you'll learn a step by step blueprint on how I did it!

FAST START BLUEPRINT

Before we get started, let me give you a 10,000 ft overview of the whole process.

It's pretty simple actually; it's just a 7 step system that you can repeat over and over again until you hit your income goal.

For now, don't even think about the $10,000/month mark…heck, don't even think about the $1,000 goal.

For now, just think about your first dollar! Once you made that first dollar, you can go to the next level which is $10, then $1,000, then $500 and so on.

The Blueprint

1 - Set Up Your KDP Account

The first thing that you need to know is the basic of self publishing and the art of making money via kindle.

2 - Finding a niche

Then, you need to find a niche and make sure that it is a profitable one. This is probably the most important part of the process.

3 - Outsourcing

The next step is to find an outsourcer who will write the book for you.

4 - Your book cover

Once you have the finished book, you can't upload it yet without a cover (duhh) – this part is so important that I decided to put an entire chapter about it. One of the biggest differences between a crappy non-selling book and the best sellers out there, besides the content, is almost always the cover.

5 – Uploading Process

The next step is the process of uploading your book. This chapter is not about the technical aspect of uploading, that is some elementary level info.
What I'm going to reveal to you are the things that you should do to make sure that your book will sell even w/o much marketing! But of course, the more marketing you do – the more it will sell.

6 - Marketing your books

Once you have your book uploaded and optimized for sales, it's time to do some promotions for your book. I'm going to give you the best ways to market your books and the exact free (or cheap) resources to do it.

Start the Engine

All right, you now know the entire process of making money via kindle publishing.
It's time to start the engine and let's go for a ride.
It's going to be a fun one, I promise.

Chapter 1 - Set Up Your KDP account

Before you start with the actual process, you need to register for a free account on kdp select.

https://kdp.amazon.com/

Sign in with your Amazon account

Sign in

Not Red?

Click here to sign in as different user.

You will be signed in using our secure server

You're gonna need some information like your bank account, tax forms and other stuff.

PAYMENT METHOD

One of the frequently asked questions I'm getting is "how do I get paid?"

You're gonna need a U.S. Bank account if Amazon doesn't accept payments in your country.

If you're in the U.S., then you really don't have to worry about anything at all.

However, for international publishers, I recommend that you use payoneer.com

They charge only 1% of the total money transferred and they are easy to work with.

To register for an account, you can go to this link.

PAYONEER FREE ACCOUNT

Yes, I'm an affiliate and I will make a gazillion dollars if you sign up, just kidding, I'll probably make $25 if you sign up through that link. I don't even care if you use it, I love that company and they really helped me a lot in my business.

Once, you got all of those set up and have a verified account, it’s time to do the nitty gritty work that will guarantee as a hefty profit.
It’s time to find our profitable niche.

Chapter 2 – Finding niches and keywords

Now the real work begins.
The good news is, it's not as hard as you think it is.
I'll show you 5 of the most effective ways to research a niche. You can choose to do only 1 or you can combine them to get even more detailed research.

The Importance of Research

It doesn't really matter how great your book content is if there is no market for that book! Even if you have the best content on cat juggling, if only 3 people are searching for it on Amazon, then it's safe to assume that you won't make a lot of money through that book.
I'm putting a lot of content in this chapter because I know how important it is in order to make money from your books.
Simply put, crappy niche = crappy sales.
In fact, if you put a lot of effort in this part, then half the "marketing" has already been done for you.
Gary Halbert, a copywriting legend once said, and I'm rephrasing here.
"If you only give me one business advantage, I will always choose "a hungry buying audience"
Choosing the right niche is like selling water on the desert!
That's the biggest advantage I can ever think of, so make sure that you follow my instructions and spend some time researching your niche.

5 ways to choose a niche/topic

These techniques work whether you want to outsource fiction or non-fiction, you just have to make sure that there is a market for that niche.

1 - Google keyword planner

One of the first step I always take when researching a niche is I use Google Keyword Planner, just to have an idea of the market size.

Let's say I want to outsource a book about "office productivity", what I will do is I'll go to https://adwords.google.com/KeywordPlanner

and search for my keyword.

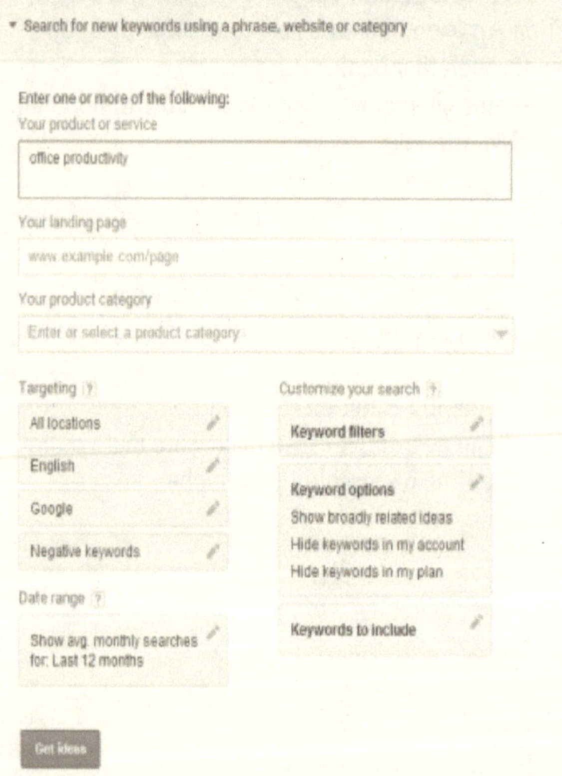

I'll look at some keywords and confirm if there are people searching for keywords related to my topic.

For my example, it looks like that there are a lot of people searching for office productivity. This means it could be a great niche for our books

Here are some keywords I gathered from this research, save this information because you're gonna need it on the "uploading process".

Ad group: **Increase Productivity**

18 of 34 ad group ideas

Download | Add all (13)

Keyword (by relevance)	Avg. monthly searches	Competition	Suggested bid	Ad impr. share	Add to plan
how to increase productivity	1,600	Low	$6.75	–	
increasing productivity	590	Low	$4.54	–	
increase productivity	1,300	Low	$6.73	–	
ways to increase productivity	260	Low	$5.44	–	
increased productivity	320	Low	$3.35	–	
how to increase employee productivity	170	Low	$0.45	–	
increase office productivity	30	Low	–	–	
increasing productivity in the workplace	110	Low	–	–	
increase employee productivity	110	Low	$22.77	–	
how to increase office productivity	20	Low	–	–	
how can productivity be increased	90	Low	$9.02	–	

2 - Google Trends

If you're not satisfied with your research, you can also use a tool called Google Trends which shows you a graph of the ups and downs of searches of your keyword.

https://www.google.com/trends/

Here's an example, when you type "office productivity".

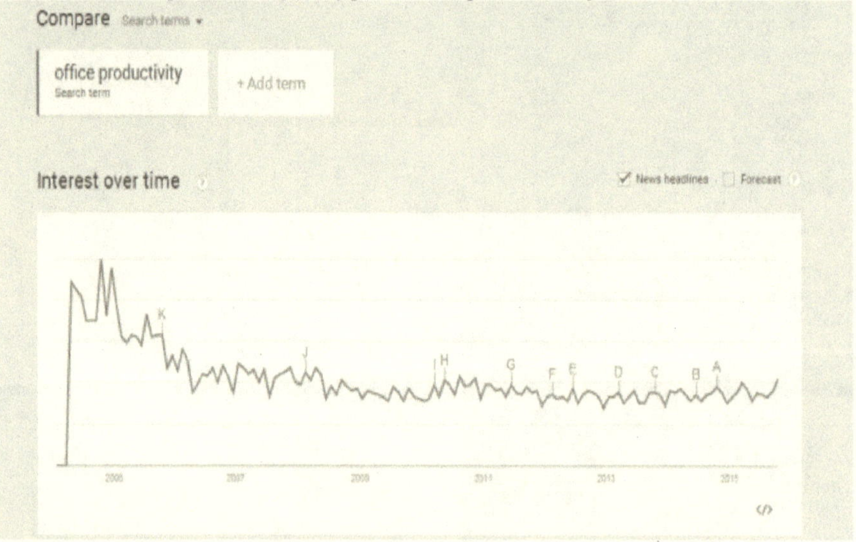

It looks like the searches are consistent – this is great news. We don't want a book that only sells during Christmas or at any given season. We want to sell it all year long.

Overall, I want to see a graph like the one above.

If you see this one instead...

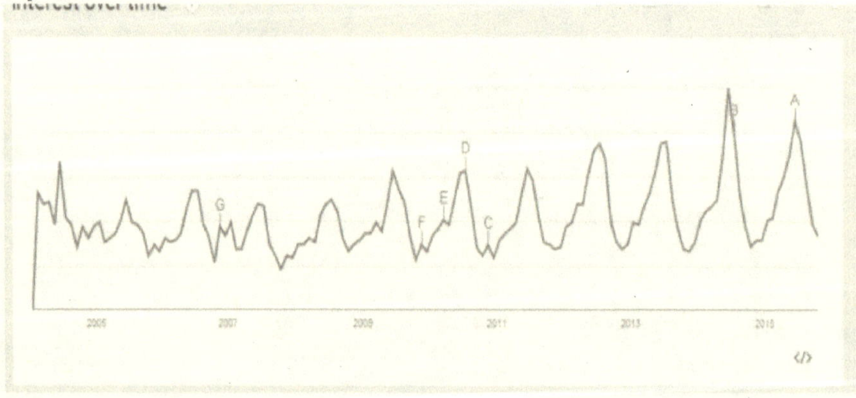

Then try to evaluate and analyze why it is only getting searches for that month. I usually avoid niches with this kind of graph, but that doesn’t mean that you will not make money on that niche. In fact, you can make a killing online just by following the trends and writing (or outsourcing) your book in that niche.

The choice is totally up to you.

3 – The Romance Category

I'm flat out giving you my most favorite niche.

If you're lazy and you don't want to do any kind of research at all, then just choose the romance category and use this method of finding a sub-category.

Go to Amazon.com and look for kindle e-book best-sellers.

Amazon Best Sellers

Our most popular products based on sales. Updated hourly.

‹ Any Department
‹ Kindle Store
Kindle eBooks
Arts & Photography
Biographies & Memoirs
Business & Money
Children's eBooks
Comics & Graphic Novels
Computers & Technology
Cookbooks, Food & Wine
Crafts, Hobbies & Home
Education & Teaching
Engineering & Transportation
Foreign Languages
Health, Fitness & Dieting
History
Humor & Entertainment
Law
Lesbian, Gay, Bisexual & Transgender eBooks
Literature & Fiction
Medical eBooks
Mystery, Thriller & Suspense
Nonfiction
Parenting & Relationships
Politics & Social Sciences
Reference
Religion & Spirituality
Romance
Science & Math
Science Fiction & Fantasy
Self-Help

Best Sellers in Kindle eBooks

Top 100 Paid Top 100 Free

1. LOOK INSIDE! Make Me: A Jack Reacher Novel by Lee Child (672) Kindle Edition $14.99

2. LOOK INSIDE! Never Smile at Strangers by Jennifer Jaynes (933) Kindle Edition $4.99

3. LOOK INSIDE! The Martian: A Novel by Andy Weir (16,804) Kindle Edition $7.99

4. LOOK INSIDE! The Girl in the Spider's Web: A Lisbe... by David Lagercrantz

5. LOOK INSIDE! The Good Neighbor by A. J. Banner (2,174)

6. LOOK INSIDE!

The Prettiest One: A Thriller by James Hankins (277)

Now, go to Romance category.

So how do we choose a sub-genre? (most call it sub-category, it's the same). Just choose any and go to the top 21-40

So I'll then click on the top 22-30 and look at the sales ranking.
If they are under 3,000, it means that they are doing a minimum of 70-100 sales a day.

I only want books that are doing these numbers of sales.

Why? Because I know that I'm still going to make money even if I'm not at the 1st page.

I don't have to have a marketing platform or be an establish author to make money on this sub-genre.

I even dig deeper and look at the top 97.

96.

Once Upon a Shifter: 10 Book PNR Bund...
by Kim Fox
(28)
Kindle Edition
$0.99

97.

Bear's Claim: BBW Paranormal Shape Sh...
by Natalie Kristen
(4)
Kindle Edition
$2.99

98.

Hunt the Darkness (Guardians of Etern...
by Alexandra Ivy
(151)
Kindle Edition
$1.99

99.

Make Him Purr: A Paranormal BBW Werep...
by Anya Nowlan
(71)
Kindle Edition
$0.99

100.

Taming the Monster: A Taming the Alph...
by Mandy M. Roth
Release Date: October 13, 2015
Kindle Edition
$0.99

Even at top 97, this book is still doing around 100+ sales a day!

Lending: Enabled
Enhanced Typesetting: Enabled
Amazon Best Sellers Rank: #1,179 Paid in Kindle Store (See Top 100 Paid in Kindle Store)
#17 in Kindle Store > Kindle eBooks > Romance > **Science Fiction**
#28 in Books > Romance > **Vampires**
#28 in Kindle Store > Kindle eBooks > Romance > Paranormal > **Vampires**

Would you like to **give feedback on images** or **tell us about a lower price**?

More About the Author

Another thing that you can do is to find sub-sub-genres.

The example I gave you is in the ROMANCE - > PARANORMAL category.

You can dig deeper into ROMANCE – PARANORMAL - > OTHER GENRES

And then repeat the process. Look at the second page of the top 100 and see if there are still books ranking under 3,000.

Look, vampires are really sucking the hell out of the kindle money right now. It's a good market to be in.

Without doing the research, you would think that the vampire craze is over since the end of the twilight series. Turn out that ladies still love vampires. I have no idea why. Go figure.

Also, use this tool to quickly calculate how many books are being sold at that ranking.
http://kindlepreneur.com/amazon-kdp-sales-rank-calculator/
(I am not in any way affiliated with that guy or website)

Kindle Best Seller
Calculator
Discover How Many Books An Author Is Selling By Entering Their Kindle Best Seller Rank

Kindle Best Seller
Calculator
110
Books Per Day
Try Again

4 – Amazon best-Sellers

Go to Amazon.com

Go to Kindle bestsellers and look for topic that grabs your interest.

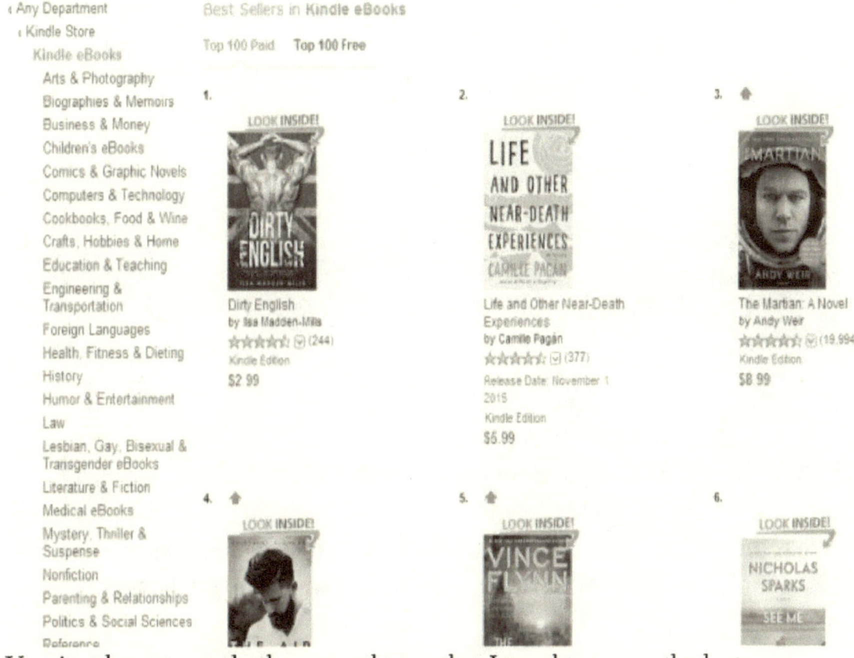

You just have to apply the same theory that I taught you on the last technique. I gave you examples on the romance niche, but you can also apply it on any other niche.

Here's another example.

I will choose the category – Thriller

And I'll look at some sub-categories

Once I got my subcategory

‹ Any Department

‹ Kindle Store

‹ Kindle eBooks

‹ Mystery, Thriller & Suspense

Suspense

Ghosts

Horror

Occult

Paranormal

Political

Psychological

Ill apply the same principle from the romance niche technique and then confirm if its top 50 has high rankings.

If it has then I'll go for this niche and find some outsourcer to write my book for me. Or if I'm knowledgeable in that topic, I will write the book myself instead.

5 – Amazon Search

If you go to Amazon's search button, you will notice that it'll give you keyword suggestions every time you put a keyword on the search bar.

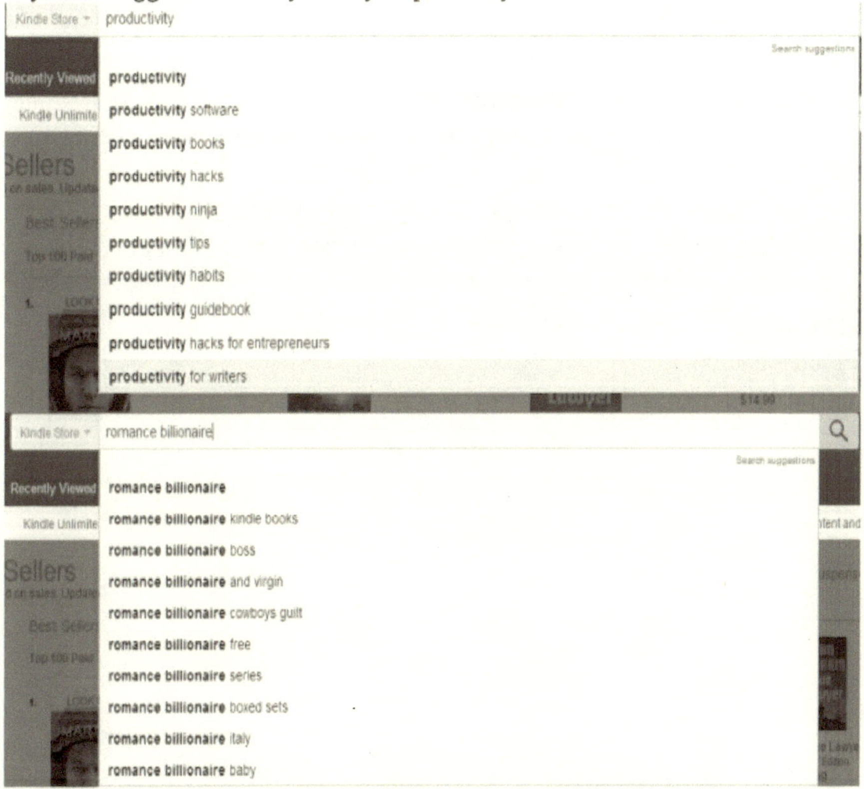

These are the exact keywords people are typing on Amazon.

Use this information and save those keywords. If people are typing it on Amazon, that means there are buyers in that market for that keyword!

This is the simplest way to do research and most publishers don't even think about it that way.

Amazon is already giving you the best keywords and niches, you just have to open your eyes and ACTUALLY use that information.

6 – Merchantwords

This is my favorite tool when researching niche or a keyword.

In fact, I never write or outsource a book unless I did some merchantwords research on it.

This tool is paid but it is cheap. It is $30 per month but you can get it for only $9 if you search for “merchantwords 60% off “on Google.

This tool lets you know the volume of searches that a keyword is getting on Amazon.com.

It is not always accurate but it can give you a pretty good idea of the volume of searches – which you can use to decide whether to push through in that niche or not.

Here’ an example on the nonfiction and fiction niche.

Procrastination…

procrastination | Search Again | In Kindle Store | Sort Highest search volume

32 results

Download as CSV

Amazon Search	Estimated Monthly Search Volume	Dominant Categories
procrastination	333,000	Kindle Store Books
procrastinating	62,500	Kindle Store Books
procrastination cure	56,500	Kindle Store Books Trade-in
procrastinators handbook	56,000	Kindle Store Books
stop procrastinating	55,000	Kindle Store Books
procrastination equation	39,500	Kindle Store Books
procrastination hypnosis	27,000	Kindle Store Books Apps & Games Audiobooks
spongebob procrastination	14,400	Kindle Store Amazon Instant Video Prime Instant Video Shop Instant Video Movies & TV
overcoming procrastination	11,200	Kindle Store Books
overcome procrastination	11,200	Kindle Store Books
procrastinate on purpose	6,400	Kindle Store Books Trade-in

Zombie apocalypse

zombie apocalypse | Search Again | In Kindle Store | Sort Highest search volume

Download as CSV

21 results

Amazon Search	Estimated Monthly Search Volume	Dominant Categories
zombie apocalypse	665,000	Kindle Store Books
minecraft zombie apocalypse	37,600	Kindle Store Books Apps & Games
i survived a zombie apocalypse	31,200	Kindle Store Books Home & Kitchen
zombie apocalypse 2	6,400	Kindle Store Books
zombie apocalypse survival guide	4,500	Kindle Store Books Trade-In
zombie apocalypse minecraft	4,000	Kindle Store Books Apps & Games
surviving the zombie apocalypse	4,000	Kindle Store Books
apocalypse zombie	2,000	Kindle Store Books Trade-In
zombie apocalypse books	1,600	Kindle Store Books
surviving zombie apocalypse	1,500	Kindle Store Books
the coming zombie apocalypse	800	Kindle Store Books
zombie apocalypse preparation	500	Kindle Store Books

If that keyword + other related keywords is getting at least 40,000 overall, I'll choose that niche and start doing some job posting about the project.

Chapter 3 – Outsourcing Your Book

So you got your niche? Awesome.

The next step is to hire someone to write your book.

I would usually pay $60-$100 for a 15,000 - 20,000 word book. That will usually be at 80+ pages.

Then you can price that at .99 to $2.99.

I recommend that you use UPWORK.COM

Here's how I would post an ad for my books.

Please don't copy-paste this template. I suggest that you edit the words and add some details that are important to you.

TEMPLATE:

Job Title

NATIVE ENGLISH ROMANCE Writer NEEDED - Pitch Me Your Series of Stories

Type of work needed

Writing & Translation > Creative Writing

Job Description

NATIVE ENGLISH WRITERS!

I am looking for 3 to 5 Romantic stories written in a series, between 20,000 words each. There will be a lot of creative freedom in this project do to the fact that I do not have a specific plot or outline. The story will be up to you. I prefer to stay away from the more explicit erotica, but spicy love scenes are welcome and encouraged. If quality is good more work is guaranteed for a LONG time to come.

- Do you have a GRIPPING Romance fictional story inside of you that you are dying to write about and have me publish to Amazon Kindle?

- IMPORTANT - This MUST be unique content and a unique story line. NO part of your story should be found ANYWHERE else. Not even on your own blogs or in other books, magazines, etc.

- Your story MUST be in the ROMANCE genre

- You should be an experienced fiction writer, good at developing characters, good at writing compelling story lines (compelling beginning to end is especially important in a short story), and able to show me other publications of your other works.

- NOTE - You should also be very adept at writing a CLIFF HANGER at the end of your story. The Reason? Think soap operas / daytime dramas / "The Young and The Restless"! One show leads into the next with a series of cliff hangers that makes the audience HAVE to watch the next episode.

...In other words, if this book does reasonably well, I will keep bringing you back to write more "episodes"! (ie - to keep adding/writing more books in your short story series!)

- YOUR name will not appear on the book. full ownership, royalties and rights stay with me

================

Detailed Requirements:

Written by a NATIVE English speaker

ORIGINAL WORK - plagiarism not tolerated

A font size of 12 points

Times new roman font type

SINGLE spaced

With margins no more than 1 inch on all sides (left, right, to, bottom)

(MANDATORY) - I also need you to include a 2-4 paragraph sales summary / description of your story, that teases/entices readers to buy

By applying/accepting this job you agree this is a WORK FOR HIRE situation. This is ghostwriting so you will own no rights to the work or parts of the work and you understand/agree your name will not appear anywhere on/in the work, nor can you share/sell/give away the work at any time.

****Please also attach a sample of your work in your reply to this message.

Thank you for taking a look at this project and I look forward to developing a long lasting working relationship with you

Regards,
YOUR NAME

The most important parts to take note are the following:

Note: This may seem a lot but they are really important so you just have to take note of the following details. Just make sure that you put all of this in your job posting.

A - The number of words that you want for your story

B - Point out that stories are theirs to create

C - Story is in Romance Genre or whatever sub-genre you chose

D - He/she must have experience

E - Let them show you their portfolio

F - Review the detailed requirements again in the body of the description.

G - Written by a native English speaker.

H - Original work only- plagiarism not acceptable.

I - Font size-12 points

J - Times New Roman font type

K - SINGLE spaced

L - Margins no more than 1 inch on all sides (left, right, top, bottom)

M - Require a 2-4 paragraph summary/description for sales and promotion.

N – How long before they finish the project

Once you got some job proposal, evaluate them by looking at their past works and how fast they respond to your questions.

I usually choose someone who has experience on the exact sub-genre that I chose. If there are no applicants that did the exact same genre, choose someone who has the most relevant experience. (assuming of course that you like their stories, writing style etc.)

Proofreading, Formatting

Once you got your book, review it and if it looks like it is ready for publishing – it's time to format the book.

You can also include the formatting part on the job description itself when you post on upwork. If you did that, then you can skip this step already.

The easiest way I know to properly format your book is via FIVERR.

It's fast and it's cheap.

Is it perfect? Well, not all the time. But it doesn't really matter. The most important part is to get you moving and then just fix little dinky things along the way.

The faster you get the book LIVE on kindle, the more money you'll make.

You just have to go to Fiverr and look for book formatting and proofreading.

Then choose one who will do it for $5-$10.

DONE.

Seriously, don’t make this part complicated.

Chapter 4 – Book Covers

Your book cover will have a huge impact in your sales.

This is where most self-published people messed up.

So they finish a book, put their heart and soul into it and they do the cover themselves just to "save money". Big mistake. Unless you're a Photoshop expert or you're absolutely broke, try to move away from designing your own shit.

Whether you like it or not, your book will always be judged by its cover, so you might as well use an amazing one.

A good cover shouldn't cost you much; $100-$300 cover is acceptable and will usually give you a bunch of covers to choose from. If you want a more premium cover, it would cost you from $200-$1,000+.If you're broke, then use Fiverr – this is especially fine if you are publishing a non-fiction book which requires less design for the book cover.

What does a great cover look like?

The answer is, it depends.

Your covers will always depend on the market and the current covers available in the market.

There's a difference between a cover that sells and a cover that impresses.

IMHO, these are the most important aspects of a great cover.

A – It must stand out

You can't have a cover that already looks like the ones your direct competitors have.

B – It must speak to your market

If you chose a good designer, they should be able to give suggestions on what covers would be best for your book. Pick something that is related to your niche and your title.

C – It should have a look and feel of premium design

This one is hard to explain but you'll always notice a premium cover when you see it

Here's how to find and select a book cover that will surely sell your book.

How to find designers

Here are 4 of the best ways to get absolutely stunning covers.

1 - 99designs.com

What I like about 99designs is that dozens and dozens of people apply for a job, they design your cover and you get to choose from a bunch of covers. If you feel like you can't choose one designer, 99designs will refund your money immediately.

2 –Upwork.com & Elance.com

You can also hire designers from Elance and Upwork. The cost may vary depending on the experience level of the freelancer. Some will charge you $50 and some will charge you $300. Before hiring a freelancer, make sure that you check their portfolio first and ask they design it themselves or work with a partner. In addition, ask them if they have previously done some covers related to your market, if they 're active in giving you suggestions, then it's safe to say that they are legit.

Also, before you hire a designer, make sure that you have a pretty good idea of what you want your design to look like. I suggest going to Amazon and randomly searching for different non-fiction topics that aren't related to your niche. You'll usually find a lot of good covers that you can copy or get inspiration from.

3 – Referrals

If you're an expert in your market, then you probably have some friends or partners who may have already published their own books. Why not ask for a referral? Tell them that you just finished your new book and you want an absolutely stunning cover for it. Also, don't be cheap about it – tell them that you are willing to pay top dollar as long as it is a premium cover.

4 – Fiverr

This should probably be your last option. Only use this one if your budget is really tight. There are many great designers in Fiverr, just make sure that you'll choose a highly-rated freelancer.

HIRING DESIGNERS

Before you hire a book cover designer, make sure that you do the following:

1 – See Samples

Look at their sample works first and see if the quality of those covers will pass your standard.

2 – Their Specialties

Most designers have some kind of "niche specialty". Sometimes, they are really good with Science fiction at the same time, quite bad at romance. Make sure that your outsourcer is matched for your niche.

3 – Does it fit the genre of your book?

Look at his/her style and make sure that it matches your book genre. Most nonfiction books are simple but enticing. Fiction covers tend to have bigger fonts compared to non-fiction books.

Chapter 5 – Uploading Process

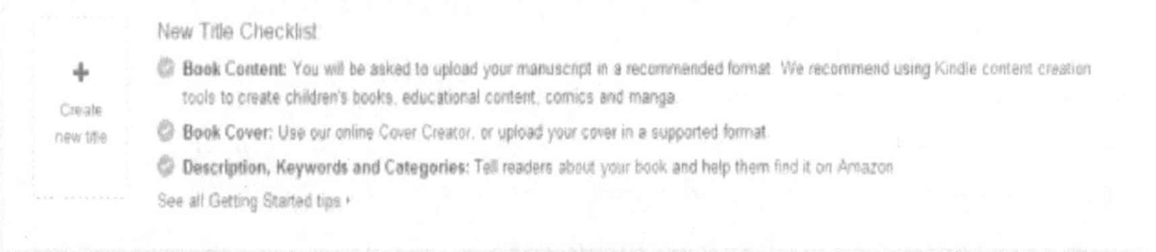

+
Create new title

New Title Checklist

- **Book Content:** You will be asked to upload your manuscript in a recommended format. We recommend using Kindle content creation tools to create children's books, educational content, comics and manga.
- **Book Cover:** Use our online Cover Creator, or upload your cover in a supported format.
- **Description, Keywords and Categories:** Tell readers about your book and help them find it on Amazon.

See all Getting Started tips ›

When you upload your book, there are things that you can do to make sure that it will sell more without much marketing.

These are your title, description, author name and your categories.

I will discuss this one by one and explain how to do it with examples.

I won't teach you the technical process since it's pretty much self explanatory.

A - Your Title

Your title will play a big part in every marketing decision that you'll make.

For my nonfiction books, I want my titles to be result based.

Say I'm writing a book about losing belly fat, then I want to target my book readers via my title.

Instead of doing something like this –

HOW TO LOSE BELLY FAT

I would do something like this -

KILL YOUR BELLY FAT: How to lose 5 lbs of belly fat, look sexier and feel better in 14 days or less.

The title above has the elements of result & time.

These all comes back to knowing your audience first.

What do people who want to lose belly fat wants to feel?

They want to lose that belly fat but there has to be a reason behind it.

In this case, they want to lose belly fat because they want to look sexier and feel better about themselves.

There is a story running in their head that if they lose that belly fat, they are more likely to get a date and will feel better about life generally.

Another aspect of this title is it is based on time.

Remember, people want instant results. I don't think it's possible to lose 5 lbs of belly fat in 3 days but 14 days is reasonable. Make this one realistic unless you can genuinely give the result in that time span.

Here's a simple formula that you can use for your title:

A - THE HOW TO FORMULAS

HOW TO (achieve result) in (time span)

KILL YOUR BELLY FAT: How to lose 5 lbs of belly fat, look sexier and feel better in 14 days or less.

HOW TO (achieve result) in (time span) without (the pain of doing it)

KILL YOUR BELLY FAT: How to lose 5 lbs of belly fat, look sexier and feel better in 14 days or less.... Without starving yourself to death.

HOW TO (achieve result) that doesn't suck.

How to write a book that doesn't suck

B - THE ART OF...THE SCIENCE OF ...Formula

I don't know what's up with the title THE ART/SCIENCE of _____, but it seems to be working really well.

If you have something that can be broken down as an art/science, then use this formula.

E.g.

The Art of Getting Rich

The Science of Making Friends

C - ________ Secrets

People love secrets.

You can also use them in your title as long as you do it right.

For this formula, you just have to put your topic in front of the word secret. And voila! You have a great title. You can also combine the HOW TO formula with this to get better results.

ONLINE TRAFFIC SECRETS: How to get 10,000 website visitors in 21 days or less...without spending a single dollar online.

B - Description

The description of your book also has a huge effect on its amazon search engine rankings. Amazon also considers the words that you are using in your description box.

Let's say you wrote a book about YOUTUBE MARKETING. If you have some keywords in your description related to YOUTUBE, then Amazon will give you better search engine rankings. Just like in normal Google SEO, if you have keywords related to your main topic, you'll get rewarded.

We call these keywords LSI.

I'll be honest, I don't really try to game the system when it comes to putting description.

I simply follow this formula for 99% of my books.

Here's a simple formula that you can use to craft a simple but effective sales description.

1 – Call out your target Market

2 – Tease the result

3 – Tell them about the problem

4 – Show them what they will learn in your book

5 – Call to action

This is the simplest way I know to sell a book.

There are other things that you can try to add. But for the basics, these 5 shall always be included in your book description.

1 – Call out your target Market

Let's use my co-author's book "25 Ways to Choose Nonfiction Book Idea"

The first thing he did was call out his target market. There are subtle ways to do this but for this book, he literally called them out.

Attention: Kindle Publishers Who Are Not Making Enough Income From Their Books

2 – Tease the result

Another thing that you can do is tease a little bit on what result they will get if they chose to buy the book. What is the result that they SHOULD strive for?

Ask any full-time kindle publisher, what is the most important first step to a successful book...and He will tell you that it's all about Choosing a Profitable Niche Idea

3 – Tell them about the problem

The next thing that he did was he twisted the knife a little bit and tell them about the big problem.

It doesn't matter if you're the best or worst writer in the world...

If there is no market for your book, I'm afraid that you will NOT make money

4 – Show them what they will learn in your book

Then he made a simple bulleted list of what they will learn inside the book.

Inside you'll learn:

How to choose a profitable topic... so you don't have to waste a single second writing your book

The exact 7 step system to go from idea to published in 60 days or less

What to do if you absolutely hate writing but still want a published book

How to map-out your book from start to finish

How to outline like a pro (this is the secret to writing a book fast!

Why Shitty first drafts are acceptable... in fact, encourage.

The importance of book covers and why it will make or break your book sales

How to increase sales even before you publish! - the secret is in the uploading process

5 – Call to action

The final step was to let them decide whether they want to stay in their current position or if they want to move forward and change their results.

Friend, stop working too damn hard for a book that will never sell!

Learn how to choose a profitable niche today!

NO RISK INVOLVED with 100% Money Back Guarantee Backed Up by Amazon

Scroll Up, Click the Buy Button and Download Your Copy Today!

You can copy this template if you want though I recommend that you change your wording and try to add your own voice into it.

For fiction writers, it could be a little different since most fiction put blurbs.

If you want to get amazing ideas for your fiction description, I suggest that you look at Stephen King's books.

EXAMPLE:

This book is about, horror, suspense and thrillers.
Look at the words inside the description.
It has keywords like:
Intensely, suspenseful, obsession, book – all of them building the case that this is a book about horror and suspense.
It's a little bit more complicated with fiction, but hopefully, I hope you get what I mean. The best way to learn this (for fiction) is to look at famous authors books and read their Amazon product (book) page.

C - Author, Editor, Illustrator

Not many authors – especially traditional ones – will do this technique.
It's a little bit shady in a way, but definitely not illegal or immoral.
In the uploading process, you'll see this tab.

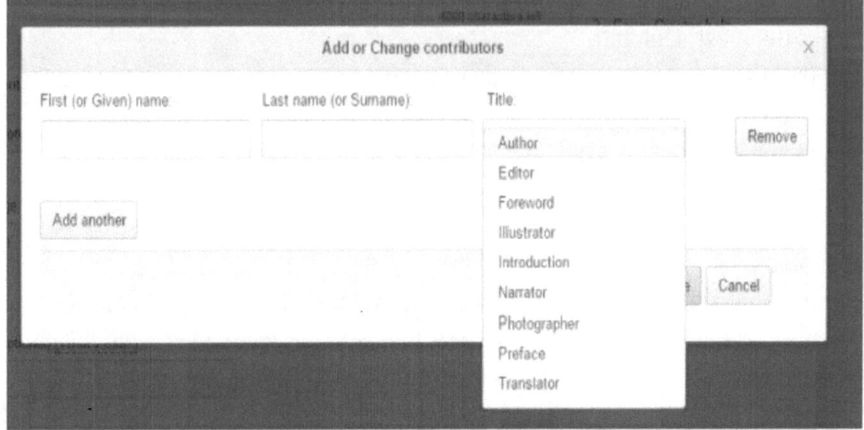

What you can do is to add your keywords in some of these tabs.
So instead of just putting your name on the AUTHOR tab, you'll add keywords related to your book on other spaces like EDITOR, ILLUSTRATOR etc.
Here's an example for a procrastination book.

Add or Change contributors ×

First (or Given) name:	Last name (or Surname):	Title:	
[redacted]	[redacted]	Author	Remove
StopProrastinationMedia	DowhatyouneedtodoInc	Illustrator	Remove
TimeManagementTips	Media	Photographer	Remove

Add another

Save Cancel

As I said, it's a little bit shady and maybe unprofessional for some people.
I don't do this in most of my books, but it does help in getting more traffic and higher Amazon search results.
For this book, I'll probably do it. Just for test results sake.

D - Categories

Most people don't have a freaking clue on what category to put their books in.
Sometimes, the smartest way to do it, is just to choose what category fits your books the most, Duhhhh.
But the truth is, most categories are just too damn competitive. That's why you need to get smart when choosing your book category.
When you're choosing your category, try to diversify as much as possible.
This really isn't that hard to do, since you only have 2 choices for your category.
Example:
For my books about SEO, in the past I just put it under the COMPUTER category. What a stupid mistake. I didn't understand my market back then.
What I realize is that most people looking for SEO information are affiliate marketers, businessman, online marketers etc.

So instead of putting my books on just the category of
WEB -> Search Engines
WEB -> Blogs

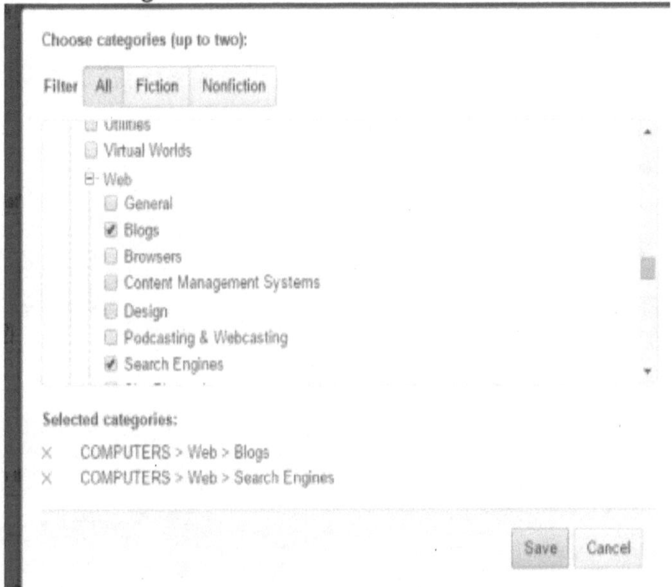

I now change the BLOG category into the HOME BASED BUSINESS category.

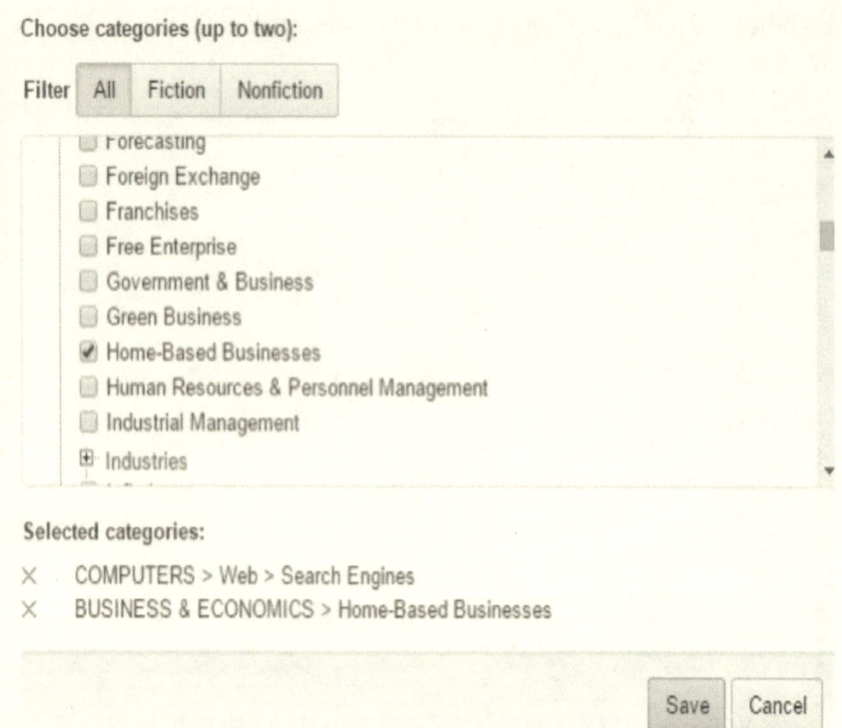

By doing this, I'll get more readers and more book buyers from different categories (buy with same purpose – which in this case is to learn SEO). Again, you have to understand the mindset behind your readers. Who are they? What do they like to search for? What other books do they read?

Another example: for fiction

Say you are writing about American soldiers fighting in the sea, then their ships got wrecked, then they got captured by pirates…on and on. Depending on your story, some categories that come to mind are the combination of:

FICTION > War and Military
FICTION > Science Fiction > Action & Adventure

Or
FICTION >Science Fiction > Action & Adventure
FICTION > Sea Stories
Or
FICTION >Science Fiction > Action & Adventure
FICTION > Ghost

(cause the pirate could be ghost like on the Pirate of the Caribbean)
Fiction is a whole different animal compared to non-fiction, so you have to get creative with it.

E - Keywords

When you upload your book, there will be an option to put 7 keywords related to your book.

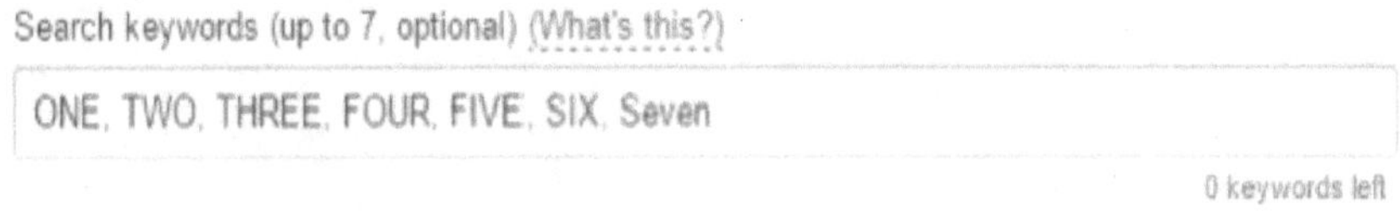

What most people do is just put 7 keywords that comes up on their minds and they're done.
We will use Google keyword tool (because we're not that stupid to not take advantage of this feature)
Let's use the zombie apocalypse example again.
If you're writing a book about ZOMBIE, then you can search for keywords related to it.

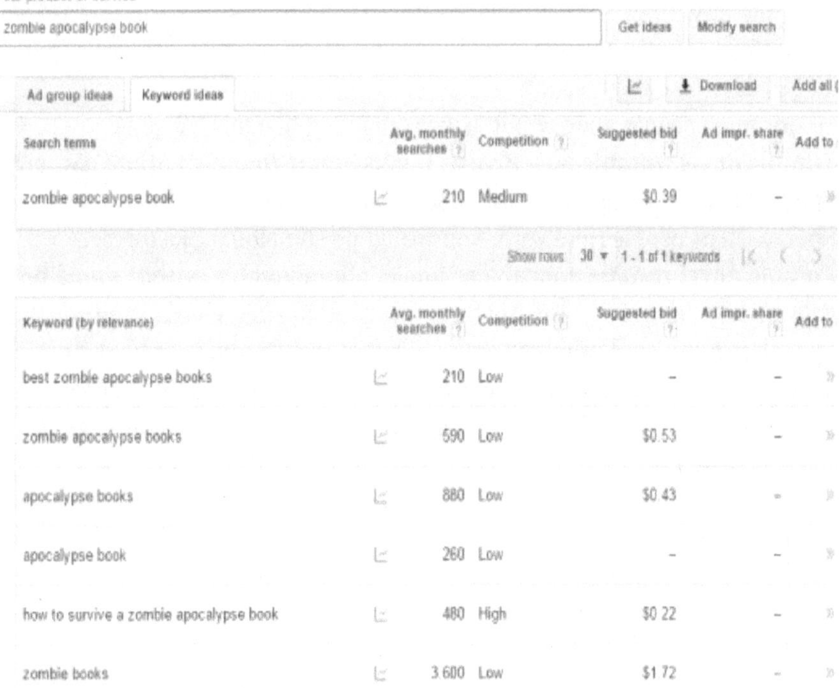

Search terms	Avg. monthly searches	Competition	Suggested bid	Ad impr. share	Add to
zombie apocalypse book	210	Medium	$0.39	-	»

Keyword (by relevance)	Avg. monthly searches	Competition	Suggested bid	Ad impr. share	Add to
best zombie apocalypse books	210	Low	-	-	»
zombie apocalypse books	590	Low	$0.53	-	»
apocalypse books	880	Low	$0.43	-	»
apocalypse book	260	Low	-	-	»
how to survive a zombie apocalypse book	480	High	$0.22	-	»
zombie books	3,600	Low	$1.72	-	»

Keyword (by relevance)	Avg. monthly searches	Competition	Suggested bid	Ad impr. share	Add to plan
how to survive a zombie apocalypse	12,100	Low	$0.32	-	»
zombie apocalypse quiz	9,900	Low	$0.12	-	»
zombie apocalypse survival	6,600	Low	$0.95	-	»
zombie apocalypse game	12,100	Low	$1.08	-	»
is a zombie apocalypse possible	880	Low	-	-	»
zombie apocalypse movie	2,400	Low	$0.24	-	»
zombie apocalypse survival guide	2,400	Low	$0.76	-	»
zombie apocalypse store	2,400	Low	$0.16	-	»

I will then use these keywords in the uploading process.

But instead of just choosing 7 keywords, I will use as much as I can slip into the Amazon keyword feature.

So, for most people, they would have something like this: (7 keywords)

Zombie novel, zombie apocalypse, books about zombie, author name, book title author name, zombie books, zombie book

For the smart people (like you), you would do something like this:

Zombie novel zombie apocalypse books about zombie author name book title author , name zombie books zombie book, surviving a zombie apocalypse the walking dead rick grimes daryl Dixon, best books related to walking dead, prepper novel books world war z 2015 2011 2012, places to survive movie paperback, amc tv walkingdead zombie gear prepper gears

You simply input more keywords and put the comma on different places. It still counts as 7 keywords but you get to target more keywords! This means more eyeballs on your book listing.

Chapter 6 – Marketing Your Books

Once you got your book published, you still have to promote your books if you really want to make more money off of it.

Here are 5 of the best FREE ways to promote your book.

1 - Create your own blog

Most successful authors I know have some kind of blog or website where they get to post content or videos for their audience to consume.

And why not, right? It's cheap and it's easier than ever to create one.

Yes, it does take some hard work to put content every single week (day) but if you are serious in growing your audience, then a blog is definitely a must.

It would take me another book to discuss everything about blogging but here are the steps that I would take if I chose this as a marketing outlet.

1 – Choose and register a domain name. I recommend that you use your name or your company name.

2 – Set up your hosting account. You can choose either Hostgator or Bluehost. If you're broke (like me when I was just getting started), then you can use 1 dollar hosting. You can find them by doing a simple Google search.

3 – Choose a theme for your blog. I'm not really big on theme. I like simple websites with white background and simple interface. It's your choice if you want to go with a simple website or a more stylistic one.

Here are some examples from two of the most famous business bloggers in the world.

- Seth godin & Tim Ferriss

Tim's blog.

http://fourhourworkweek.com/blog/

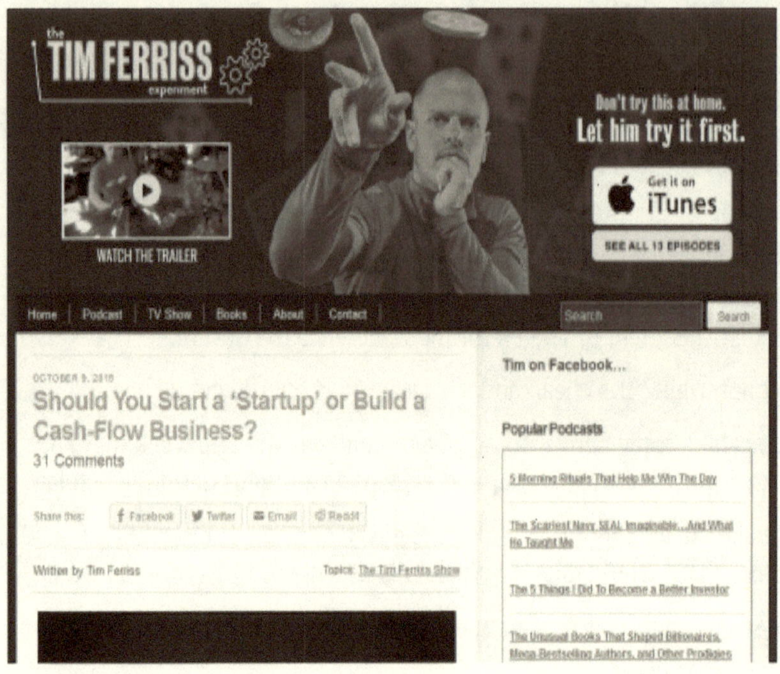

Seth's blog.

http://sethgodin.typepad.com/

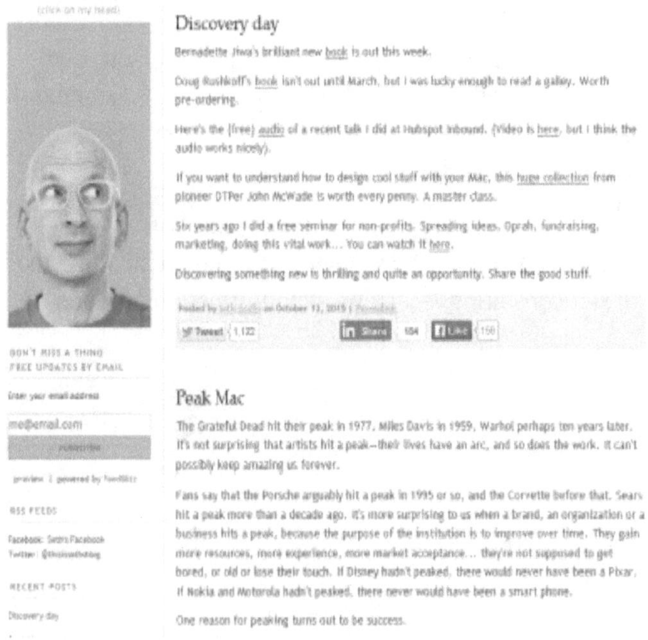

Discovery day

Bernadette Jiwa's brilliant new book is out this week.

Doug Rushkoff's book isn't out until March, but I was lucky enough to read a galley. Worth pre-ordering.

Here's the (free) audio of a recent talk I did at Hubspot Inbound. (Video is here, but I think the audio works nicely).

If you want to understand how to design cool stuff with your Mac, this huge collection from pioneer DTPer John McWade is worth every penny. A master class.

Six years ago I did a free seminar for non-profits. Spreading ideas, Oprah, fundraising, marketing, doing this vital work... You can watch it here.

Discovering something new is thrilling and quite an opportunity. Share the good stuff.

Peak Mac

The Grateful Dead hit their peak in 1977, Miles Davis in 1959, Warhol perhaps ten years later. It's not surprising that artists hit a peak—their lives have an arc, and so does the work. It can't possibly keep amazing us forever.

Fans say that the Porsche arguably hit a peak in 1995 or so, and the Corvette before that. Sears hit a peak more than a decade ago. It's more surprising to us when a brand, an organization or a business hits a peak, because the purpose of the institution is to improve over time. They gain more resources, more experience, more market acceptance... they're not supposed to get bored, or old or lose their touch. If Disney hadn't peaked, there would never have been a Pixar. If Nokia and Motorola hadn't peaked, there never would have been a smart phone.

One reason for peaking turns out to be success.

Both blogs works and have huge followers even though they have different blog styles. One is design focused and one is a simple plain looking blog.

4 – Choose what kind of blog you want to have. Do you want a pure text only blog? A video blog? Both?

You can also use your blog as another platform for your podcast. You can put downloadable mp3's there and let them say their thoughts on the comment section.

5 – Decide on how would you reach more people?

Here are some ways to get traffic for free or cheaply.

A – Your books. Always put your website link on your books.

B – Google SEO. Rank your keywords on the 1st page of Google.

C – Facebook Ads. Most people think that FB ads are expensive. Well they aren't, as long as you track your expenses, cut your losses and expand with the winner ads.

D – Affiliate. If you decided to create a product, you can have your own readers as your affiliate and let them promote it in exchange of a commission. You'll basically make money and drive traffic without even trying to promote. You let others do the work for you.

6 – Monetize your blog. Do you want to make money purely from book sales? By having a blog, you could expand your reach and create more than just books. You can sell consulting, coaching and information products and online courses.

2 - Blogging platforms

Between the blog and other social media platforms, there are websites called blogging platforms where you can share your content with the mass audience.

It's not easy to get accepted, but if you have amazing content and insights – then this would be beneficial to you.

The good news is that these websites are large and influential and are always looking for contributors. They would often give away accounts for writers and will let you post as much content as you like to.

Some of the big blogging platforms are:

The Huffington Post

Business Insider

Medium

The Verge

Guidelines to Get Accepted

1 – Focus on solution.

Writing about a certain problem is great but you also have to give the solution to this problem. Don't just complain about it, do something about it instead. Sites like HuffingtonPost like this kind of content.

2 – Original.

Never ever copy somebody else's work. You can get inspiration from them but never copy paste anything.

One awesome thing about these platforms is that they allow you to repurpose the content that is already in your blog.

3 – Sharable

Are there people interested in that topic? Do you think normal everyday people would be interested in what you have to say and will share it to their friends?

If it's boring and uninteresting – then forget about your article and write a new one.

4 – Current News Event

If you can somehow tie your topic with some current news event, it would be a plus - though not really necessary.

Resources to read:

http://www.theverge.com/write-for-the-verge

http://thewritelife.com/how-to-write-for-the-huffington-post/

https://www.quora.com/How-do-you-become-a-writer-for-the-Huffington-Post

http://www.businessinsider.com/contribute-to-business-insider

http://www.businessinsider.com/stephen-king-on-how-to-write-2014-8

3 - Info Graphics

These are visual representations of your ideas relating to your book.

They should be visually compelling and informative.

What I like about info graphic is their ability to get noticed fast. Which means they are likely to go viral compared to a blogpost.

Here are some examples of info graphics.

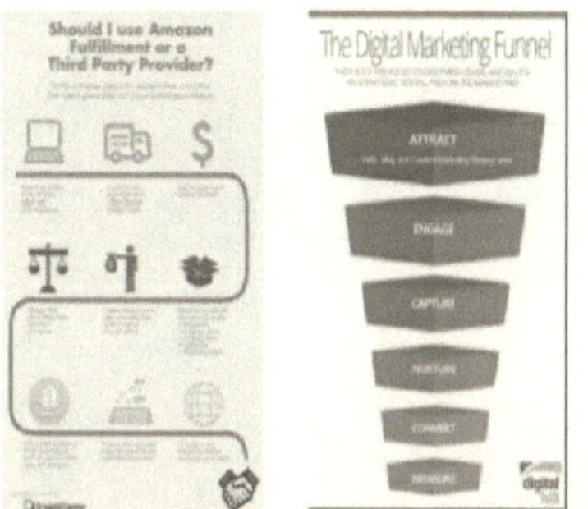

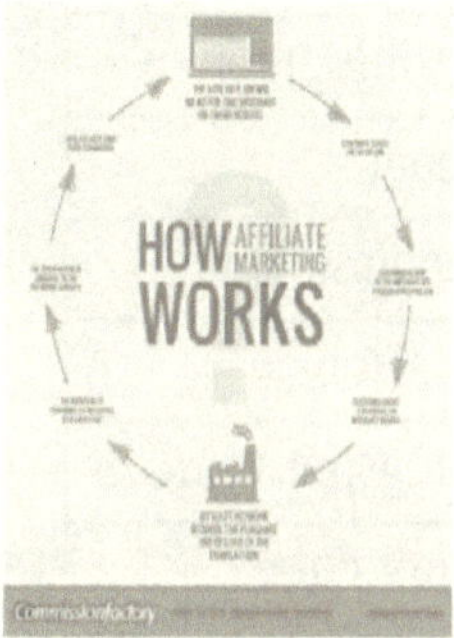

(These infographics have beautiful design, content driven, and/or data driven and the link to their website or the creator's name is included)

Two Ways to Do It

You can either

1- Create and design one for yourself

2- Hire someone to do it for you

I recommend that you just hire someone to do it for you. There are fiverr gigs that would accept to do it for you for a measly $5.

Another awesome things about infographics is they can be put pretty much anywhere. This gives you more leverage and exposure for your website or your book.

If you want to, you can even publish an e-book with the collections of info graphics as your main content. In addition, you can also add these info graphics as part of the content of your blog.

Here are some resources to get you started.

For free infographic creation

http://piktochart.com/

For Infographic Submission

http://visual.ly
http://www.slideshare.net/
http://www.infographicsshowcase.com/
http://www.infographicsarchive.com
http://www.reddit.com/r/infographics
http://www.nerdgraph.com
http://www.loveinfographics.com
http://submitinfographics.com
http://theinfographics.blogspot.com
http://infographixdirectory.com/
http://infographicsite.com
http://infographaholic.tumblr.com
http://www.infographicpost.com

4 - Live Videos - Google Hangout or Webinars

Doing these live videos wouldn't really cost you much so I recommend that you do this. I'll be the first to admit that doing a Google Hangout or a webinar just to sell a book is a little bit of an overkill. You don't need to run a webinar to sell a book. But if you really want to connect your audience and build that "1,000 true fans" as they say, then this is the perfect outlet to use.

You're not only providing good content through these live videos, but you're also selling yourself and all your future projects as well.

This is one of the best ways to connect with your audience and build a mutual relationship.

There are 3 types of live videos that you can create.

1 – Teaching Video

You'll just explain anything from your book and give an in depth look behind your content

2 – Interview

Just like a podcast, you'll have someone as a guest and interview him.

3 – Q & A

You could also do a pure Q & A – reddit style – but instead of just interacting through text, you get to answer their questions live.

Steps to Take

Here are the basic steps to take to help you with the process of doing live videos.

1 – Choose the type of video you want to create

2 – Choose a video platform you want to use. (please see resources)

3 – Invite people to join you via a simple landing page/opt-in page

4 – Share your invite in every blogging/social media platform if you have no email list yet. You can also use reddit for this step.

5 – Make sure that you remind them to attend at a specific time and date

6 – Provide massive value and good content for your viewers

7 – Ask them to buy your book

8 – Give them bonuses; this will increase your book sales by more than 100%!

Resources to get started:

https://www.anymeeting.com/adw/Free-Webinar-Service.aspx

https://www.anymeeting.com/

https://hangouts.google.com/

5 - Draft2digital – Perma-Free

What draft2digital does is that it allows you to upload your book there and they will be the one to upload it on other platforms like kobo,nook,apple etc.

Here's how the draft2digital strategy works.

1 - You write a short book about your topic. It could be just 30-50 pages.

2 – Upload it in draft2digital and make it free.

3 – In that version of the book, don't add any Amazon url or links to your other books. Just make it free and you can leave it there forever.

4 – The next step is to upload a different version on Amazon with a link to your longer book. Amazon won't allow you to price the book for free, this is where draft2digital comes in handy. You simply email Amazon the links to all of these free books and ask them to price match your Amazon book to your Draft2digital books. I never had any problem getting perma-free while using this tactic. It's the fastest way I know to get a book perma-free on Amazon.

5 – Make sure that you put some great valuable content inside your shorter book. At the beginning and end of your book, recommend your longer book and ask them to buy and review it. This is kind of the same strategy as the first few strategies that I taught you, except that our shorter book is permanently free and it will serve as the introduction to some of our other books.

6 – (OPTIONAL) You can also outsource your shorter book if you don't want to write more content. Just be careful with the voice of the book and make sure that the content is genuinely good and readable.

Conclusion

Great job on finishing this book.

Normally, on a book conclusion, I would say something like these…

TAKE ACTION!, NEVER GIVE UP! JUST KEEP AT IT!

But since I'm feeling really lazy today, I'm just gonna assume that you already know that by not doing these things – YOU WILL NOT MAKE MONEY!

This is not a get rich quick scheme.

This is a legit way to actually earn a living online via Amazon Kindle Publishing.

If you're now ready to do those things, then close this book and get started today!

Good luck!

www.ingramcontent.com/pod-product-compliance
Lightning Source LLC
LaVergne TN
LVHW041126150826
845673LV00007B/2199

* 9 7 9 8 4 5 8 3 2 2 5 0 8 *